THE C.A.M.P.
GUIDE TO ASTROLOGY

Borgo Press Books by VICTOR J. BANIS

THE C.A.M.P. GUIDE TO ASTROLOGY

WITH THE HELP OF LADY AGATHA & JACKIE HOLMES

VICTOR J. BANIS

THE BORGO PRESS

MMXII

THE C.A.M.P. GUIDE TO ASTROLOGY

FIRST BORGO PRESS EDITION

Published by Wildside Press LLC

www.wildsidebooks.com

DEDICATION

I am deeply indebted to my friend, Heather, for all the help she has given me in getting these early works of mine reissued.

And I am grateful as well to Rob Reginald, for all his assistance and support.

CONTENTS

FOREWORD

If there's one subject almost certain to break the ice, and sometimes even bring things to a boiling point, it's the subject of Astrology. I touched upon it ever so briefly in *Sex and the Single Gay*, and was nearly deluged by remarks about my remarks. They ranged from "sock it to 'em" to "may the good fairy pooh on your gnurr."

At this point I'm probably expected to make a ringing defense of the star system, or admit that it's all a put-on. Sorry, Dux, but I'm just not going to do either. The fact is, Astrology can be useful and awesomely accurate, but if taken in the wrong light, it can be a sheer farce.

The best qualification I ever heard for Astrology is Lady Agatha's own—the stars impel, they don't compel. In other words, they nudge you into certain channels, but they don't force you. This is one of the big advantages of knowing about your astrological influences. If, for instance, you know that you have a tendency to a certain fault, you can correct it my making yourself behave otherwise.

Some people pooh-pooh any of the mystical sciences, saying that life would be worthless if everything were predetermined. Yes, I suppose it would be, if....

Try looking at it this way. Suppose the neighborhood chickens (lovely neighborhood) are playing ball outside your window, and one of the little mothers hits his ball (just one) toward your window. Now, a picture taken just then would show his big thing speeding through the air toward your bay window. At this point you could make a pretty safe prediction that the ball would shatter the window. And that's just what will happen—unless something interferes. Suppose you open the window at this moment. Or suppose one of the kiddies jumps up very high and palms the speeding muscle...excuse me, missile. You see, your prediction was perfectly accurate, but it didn't come true. Things are predetermined only as possibilities, subject to change.

What does all this mean to you? Well, Lola, if you really are up on your stars, you may see that there's a skiing accident in store for you. In that case, you just stay in bed. Like opening the window, you change the pattern of things.

Astrology has a lot to do with sex, too...practically everything does. Let's face it, we'd every one of us toss out our beads for a good man. Think of how we plot and scheme and connive just for a *nuit d'amour*. (That's French for making out.)

Well, Bessie, the stars make everything easier. They tell us all about his moods, his weaknesses—even the most important parts of his body—you see, every astrological sign influences a specific part of the body.

Yes, girls, there is one for IT, but I'm going to make you read on to find out which sign.

Now I knew someone was going to ask me what I mean by "sign." I'm leaving that up to Lady Agatha. All I wanted to do here was give you an idea or two for using what you're going to learn.

Oh, yes, there's one other reason for reading on—can you think of anything gayer than heavenly bodies?

—Jackie Holmes

INTRODUCTION

Everybody has a star to swing on, and hopefully other things as well. (Some lucky girls might even have one in Hollywood.) What we're concerned with here though is basically to deal with stars other than the Hollywood variety, so first of all we have to have a map to get us started C.A.M.P.ing through the heavens. Yes, that's heavens...plural, like in heavens to what's-her-name. There are twelve for our present purposes.

Not being prone to linger long over mechanics, unless they're cute and the two-legged variety, we'll make short work of what might be a tedious subject. So, let's consider the heavens as a great circle and divide it into equal parts, just like a clock face is divided into twelve parts by the hour divisions. Each of these twelve may then be considered to represent one of the signs of the Zodiac, which are:

Aries the Ram
Taurus the Bull
Gemini the Twins
Cancer the Crab
Leo the Lion
Virgo the Virgin

Libra the Scales
Scorpio the Scorpion
Sagittarius the Archer
Capricorn the Goat
Aquarius the Water-bearer
Pisces the Fishes

We are also taught that there are twelve types of individuals more or less corresponding to these twelve signs. For instance, if you were born in the fourth sign, Cancer—that is if the sun was in that sign when you were born, you would be one kind of person; if you were born when the sun was in Aries, the first sign, you would be another.

Of course, there are, unfortunately, finer complications that have to be taken into consideration, because certainly not all of the millions of people on the earth who were born strongly under one sign or the other are the same type individuals. If they were, then Astrology would be a simple enough study and would not warrant much minute attention. It would be rather repetitious and uninteresting too to have only twelve types of individuals. But each of the twelve signs has its own definite, distinct characteristics and those born under a particular sign reflect a great deal of its characteristics.

For instance, if you know someone who was born under the sign of Taurus, you have probably learned that that's an individual that you just don't wave a red flag in front of. Cancerians can usually be found at home—they like it there best.

They're also very fond of water (not to mention other

things), but I think that's something everybody has in common. Do you know anyone born under the sign of Libra? Well balanced and even tempered, aren't they? Except when you cross them, then look out, Louise.

It would be in order, now, to list the various signs along with the dates that correspond to each. Bear in mind, however, that these dates vary slightly from year to year, and if your birthday falls on this borderline (or cusp) you might want to check with an astrologer about your own case.

Aries the Ram—March 21st to April 19th
Taurus the Bull—April 20th to May 20th
Gemini the Twins—May 21st to June 21st
Cancer the Crab—June 22nd to July 21st
Leo the Lion—July 22nd to August 21st
Virgo the Virgin—August 22nd to September 22nd
Libra the Scales—September 23rd to October 22nd
Scorpio the Scorpion—October 23rd to November 21st
Sagittarius the Archer—November 22nd to December
    21st
Capricorn the Goat—December 22nd to January 20th
Aquarius the Water-bearer—January 21st to February
    19th
Pisces the Fishes February 20th to March 20th

There! Those are all the signs (of the Zodiac, girl— I didn't say a thing about symptoms), but I think we should say something about cusps. First of all, cusp is a four-letter word, but it's not dirty. It refers to a period of about seven days, when the influence of Gemini, for instance, is merging into that of Cancer, and Cancer still retains some vibrations (love that word) of Gemini. Anyone born in this period would possess the brilliance and versatility of Gemini and also the tenacity and loyalty of the Cancer. Briefly they are a combination of the two—and thoroughly to understand them requires taking into consideration the characteristics of both signs. People born at other times of the month need only be concerned with their own sign.

Let's not get any more complicated than this, and without further ado let's get into the analyses of each sign.

CHAPTER ONE
ARIES

MARCH 21ST THROUGH APRIL 19TH

The sign of leadership is Aries, the first sign of the Zodiac, and is ruled—if anything quite so powerful can be ruled—by Mars, an aggressive and warlike planet. This combination usually produces a courageous, enterprising, ambitious and forceful individual.

It too frequently happens that the Aries girl who has all this swinging for her will go down to defeat (who giggled?) just because all of these wonderful qualities become diverted into less constructive channels; if you know what I mean. And the finer the quality— the more readily, it seems, it becomes perverted. For instance, one of the beautiful characteristics, idealism, has inspired leaders of men (and boys) from time immemorial, but if allowed to run out of check in the Aries person enthusiasm becomes fanaticism, radicals develop from liberals and otherwise people who you'd think would know better go off half-cocked—and that's no fun.

But if you're looking for a real lover boy, one who is

a good friend and companion, the typical native of the sign of Aries with his idealism under proper control is one of the most delightful ever. And, as a lover, the Aries shines in comparison with many of his brothers (or sisters).

And you can (almost) rest assured that there is nothing common or vulgar about his feelings for sex. He is fiery, demonstrative and very passionate, but always in his heart there is admiration, even a certain amount of worshipfulness. And without this quality he is unhappy.

Aries fancies himself the protector, the knight in shining armor, the pure in heart—and nothing should be said to let him think otherwise. The business world offers a most wonderful field to the Aries person and there they may use their best Aries qualities. They have a natural executive ability, and a dynamic personality necessary to bear authority (watch one hold court some time and you'll see what I mean), and to deal with associates and subordinates.

Aries never says die. Industry is another prime quality and even the least little ribbon clerk or stenographer knows that the big prizes in the world of affairs go to those who are always on the job.

The Arien however does have a tendency to pay more attention to getting things started than to finishing them, and this is often a contributing factor to their sometimes not succeeding in business—sometimes, life itself. Aries is constantly beginning a new project—and while this makes for interest, activity and progress, unless he is one of those natives of this sign who has a certain amount of tenacity, little will be accomplished.

This scattering tendency unchecked will not only affect his business, but the naturally fine mentality of the Aries girl tends to get a bit dissipated when she finds herself with too many irons in the fire. If they would only think before they act—just count to ten (more if necessary) before tackling something new, the average Aries would be right ten times oftener. Although most of us might suffer should we become too introspective, a certain amount of it becomes the Aries.

Aries is the head sign of the Zodiac. Now, no one said anything about head jobs. As I told you, each sign is associated with a part of the anatomy. It is the sign of people who go to the top. It rules, then, naturally enough the physical head of man as well as the spiritual one. Aries people have to beware of injuries to the head and internal disorders.

Aries rules the stomach and kidneys as well, and the native of the sign would do well to be careful of ailments that settle in those parts. In later life there may be threats from paralysis and apoplexy, but fortunately the strength of Mars comes to the rescue, and with proper diet and moderate living, the Aries can be assured of living to be a dirty old man.

When the Aries person gets ready to share pots, pans and throw rugs, generally they'll find their most compatible mates under the signs of Leo or Sagittarius—and the least compatible would be those born under Cancer, Libra, and Capricorn.

Of course, these are only indications—but the natives of the first two mentioned signs are naturally sympathetic to Aries, and helpful. They should make excellent partners in business or bed. But definite rules cannot be laid down, and the best thing to do is find out all you can about your own personality as indicated by the stars, then do the same thing for the "other person."

And even though it's not nice to have it called to attention, most Aries must bear in mind that they probably have some of their virtues carried to the extreme where they become faults. Idealism may become a lack of balance, a lust for power may arise from ambition, strength may generate obstinacy; initiative may become aggression, courage, bravado, daring foolhardiness. Against this the Aries must constantly guard.

Aries is the ram, and gets ahead—even if it is necessary to butt and ram its way through. Just watch one pushing a shopping cart through the supermarket!

But let's get more specific than this and look more closely at various Aries types—you see, what part of the month you were born makes a difference too.

Those born between March 21st and March 30th—

Were born under the very first part of the very first sign of the Zodiac. If you qualify for this distinction you are a natural born pioneer girl, a real leader—and an adventuress. Your dominant planet is Mars, which rules the whole sign of Aries, and was especially powerful at the time of your birth—and thanks to its influence you should have the courage, energy and strength to fulfill your highest destiny.

The true son (or daughter as the case may be) of Mars tends to be somewhat aggressive, sometimes to the point of being antagonistic. This could arouse the opposition of others unless guarded against. Harmony at home and at work are important to the Aries, and he should strive to achieve this condition.

This is the mental type person. Witty in speech, although sometimes cynical or bitchy. Their mind moves quickly and they can't stand routine, and order takes a back seat. To get the best results from their natural executive ability they should plan their work first.

Your colors are all reds, scarlet, carmine, and crimson—you gay thing, you. Your flowers are the buttercup, hawthorne and anemone, and your stones: the amethyst, moonstone, bloodstone and diamond. If you should find your stones, flowers or colors unbecoming to you it is not necessary to wear them. If, however, you choose to wear them you will be dressing in harmony with your stars.

The Aries lover is very romantic and given to sudden enthusiasms. Quite frequently he is violent in the expressions of his affection. (I'm going out tomorrow—oh, hell, today—and find one. VJB) They seldom create an atmosphere of rest, tranquility or serenity.

These people also have a fine natural gift for political or public work. They can find success and happiness as a military leader in time of war or an executive position connected with machinery in times of peace. They are marvelous at getting enterprises started—but should strive to finish them as well.

Mars figures doubly powerful in the horoscope of these people and is a prime indicator of the choice of profession. Soldiers, chemists, surgeons, barbers, workers in steel and iron and mechanics are those most especially favored. Mostly butch types who are long on courage, aggression, initiative, boldness and executive ability.

Those born with this configuration (that has nothing to do with your girdle) tend to have problems with both the stomach and the kidneys and should avoid excessive use of sweets (the candy kind that is). Paralysis and apoplexy bother some of them later in life, but proper diet and exercise (take that any way you want to) can avoid these conditions. Injuries to the face and head can also be a problem.

The Aries of this part of the sign has the highest potential, and can be a leader. He should not miss these possibilities by being too aggressive or dictatorial. Mars is on his side!

Those born between March 31st and April 9th—

Are by no means the proverbial ninety-seven pound weaklings. The giver of life, the Sun, and the war god, Mars dominated the heavens at the time of their birth, and their sign, of course, is Aries.

The person with this combination is at the same

time a very interesting one, and one who is interested deeply in political affairs (and other affairs, too?).

That father of all the heavenly bodies (you know we'd get around to those sooner or later) tends to give these people honor, prestige (nice), celebrity (fortunately, not celibacy), position (naturally) and power. Courage, energy and strength are injected by Mars, along with fearlessness, demonstrativeness and independence; while the Sun tends to make them truthful, honest and noble.

However, on the other hand, they can be very impulsive, cynical, overly aggressive and bitchy at the drop of a bead. The degree of success in their lives depends upon how successful they are in conquering these latter qualities by the use of the former.

Their prime physical threats are from the area of the stomach and the kidneys. Careful, girls, what you eat and drink. They should get lots of exercise (the out-of-bed variety too). Pay attention to headaches—they are not so much of a problem in themselves, but are symptomatical. With the Sun and Mars so much in their favor though, their health should generally be good (real all-night swingers).

As with most Aries they possess executive ability and a tendency to be scatterbrained at the same time. They should pay more attention to getting things finished than to starting new ones—and are bored stiff with routine. They should stop occasionally and take a look at themselves, order their thoughts and their work; be less hasty in reaching conclusions and once having reached them, be even less hasty in putting them into action.

Businesses with fire and machinery connected with them should be most appealing, along with positions requiring leadership, military, political or social (you can say that they might be the queen mother of the block, if they put their minds to it).

Workers in steel and iron (that sounds like an S&M bit), surgeons, dentists (a little more of the same), barbers and chemists are likely professions for these people, along with some of the occupations ruled by the Sun such as jewelers, goldsmiths and others dealing with precious metals. Rulers and leaders (queens, dowagers?) and others in high authority are favored by the Sun's dominance here.

Their colors are yellow (are you ready for this?), brown, and blood-reds. Your flowers are hawthorne, buttercups and anemones, and your stones, chrysolite, amethyst, bloodstone and diamond.

These people should also remember that men are attracted to them by the brilliant rays of the Sun and should guard against driving them away with the over-aggressiveness of their Mars. Nobody loves a pushy Martian.

Success lies in the establishment of harmonious relations with associates, achieved by guarding against their tendency to be dictatorial. They can rule, but not when it arouses antagonism.

Those born between April 10th and April 19th—

Tend to be somewhat impulsive and over-enthusiastic. This results from the double rulership of Mars over their entire sign, Aries, and the planet of the goddess of love, Venus over this particular part of the sign. (You can imagine what's going to happen when the gods and goddesses of War and Love get together—all that bit about "all's fair in....") Well, it's true, these people are pleasure loving, gay, and love social amusement, but like poetry and art as well. Of course, anybody all that gay would love poetry, wouldn't he?

They lack not for friends, and their Venusian aspect makes them kind and generous, and gives them a conversational ability which is sparkling and clever, albeit somewhat sharp and cynical at times. They exude that particular charm known as sex appeal.

Aggressiveness is the one quality that could be their downfall, but the planet of love, Venus, tends to soften this quality somewhat and helps to overcome it. But Venus is a softener, and cannot help the Aries person over his (or her) lack of stick-to-it-iveness. They are still starters, and not finishers; pioneers and adventurers. Routine might as well be a four-letter word; they dislike it. They tend too much to scatter their energies.

They owe it to themselves to use their energies to lead, and they have a natural ability for this calling—but they could be easily led astray by their tendency toward belligerence given them by Mars, and toward indulgence in pleasure—a gift of Venus. They should avoid pettiness and quarrelsomeness and conceit.

Their colors are white, light blue, and all sorts of red; their stones, beryl, green jasper, coral, carnelian, amethyst, sapphire, and diamond; their flowers, hawthorne, buttercup, and anemone. If they wish to dress in harmony with their stars they may choose any of these jewels, flowers, and colors, but if they should find them unbecoming, it is not necessary that they do so.

The planetary influences of Mars and Venus play heavily upon the emotions and are both influential in the horoscope of people born in this part of Aries, and have a most interesting influence on the romantic nature. In this regard they tend to be less aggressive, less demanding, less quarrelsome and warlike than most Aries. They can learn to cooperate in family life and succeed brilliantly in marriage.

The vulnerable organs of Aries here are the stomach and the kidneys and they should avoid over indulgence in eating and drinking, especially sweets.

(Sweets might object, but we're talking about candy. I could go on from there with Candy and Sugar objecting in turn, too, but now the point's well made. Oh, never mind.) Anyhow, by paying attention to proper diet and exercise they can enjoy a long and vigorous life.

Occupation-wise the executive ability of these people shows best in occupations congenial to them. Mars would indicate the following: soldiers, surgeons, chemists, dentists, barbers, and iron and steel workers. And wouldn't you know that it indicates work, too, with the Army and Navy?

But the love planet cannot be denied, and Venus suggests musicians, painters, poets, singers, actors, perfumers and coutouriers, confectioners and florists. (See any of your friends here, Mary?)

In public life all Aries tend to succeed (gotta be careful about that, too) and in all military positions (uh-huh) and political ones. In positions connected with fire (they're hot little numbers) and machinery (and butch). But Venus, here may make the native more "artsy-crafty." The important thing for them to learn is not just to start something, but to be able to finish it, too.

CHAPTER TWO
TAURUS

APRIL 20TH THROUGH MAY 20TH

Taurus is a warm and friendly sign, and the people who fall under its influence tend to be warm, friendly, affectionate and passionate, but, strangely enough, not really demonstrative, at least not in these qualities.

As you all know, the various signs of the Zodiac each have their own symbol, and appropriately enough the symbol of Taurus is the Bull. Strong, and bull-headed the Taurus snorts, plunges and bellows through life intent on gaining his goal.

The Taurean is earthy, and he doesn't care who knows it. He wants what he wants and he wants it when he wants it. (And he usually gets it.)

However, not everything about the Taurus is hard; if one appeals to the softer side of their nature, and they have one, they can be very gentle.

This is most greatly evidenced in their home life— they are good home-makers and good providers, and actually much more domestic than they are romantic. They care, or at least seem to care much more for their homes than they do for their marital partner. They have much more of a paternal (or maternal) instinct than they do a mating instinct.

This by no means implies that the Taurean is not loyal in his love affairs. On the contrary, they can be, and frequently are, possessively loyal, but the saving grace here is that they will tend to express their affection in the day-to-day amenities; a fact which makes them a little less exciting a lover than natives of the more intense signs, but comfortable as a mate.

The ruling planet of Taurus is the planet of love, Venus; but even the goddess of beauty must express herself in an earthy way in this sign to bring about her effect of softening and refining. The artistry of Venus will tend more to express itself in the fields of architecture, building, landscape-gardening and interior decoration than in painting or sculpture.

The influence of Venus can give the Taurean a Ferdinand-like quality, too: peaceful, gentle and serene; qualities which make them a desirable companion in almost any relationship. It gives them an imperturbability which does not often explode as a result of having their feelings hurt—but this cannot be counted upon. Like Ferdinand, who sat on the bee, once the Taurus feels and is convinced that he is being imposed upon he can be and is a bitch-on-wheels.

On the physical side (frequently a lovely side, indeed), Taurus rules the throat. That should indicate something. Strangely enough, a great number of actors and actresses born strongly under the influence of Taurus, made their first impression on the public and reached sudden heights after the advent of talking pictures. Some people say that even today the throat plays an important part in getting ahead in the world. Taurus is frequently the sign of opera and concert singers. If you feel like a lark, or a swallow, Taurus may have something to do with it.

In the world of affairs (and I ask you is there another?) the Taurean certainly enjoys his share of success. In Astrology two of the heavenly bodies (oooh!) are known as stars of fortune. They are Jupiter, which is called the greater fortune and Venus which is known as the lesser fortune. This is by no means derogatory to the goddess of love—it's just that she's considered a little less fortunate, or perhaps fortunate in a different way than Jupiter, the chief of the gods and the god of weather and the heavens. Their success will chiefly lie in cooperating with Venus (pardon the pun, but I'd love to) in the earthy realm of Taurus. Feet-on-the-ground is the key word.

Strong-as-a-bull. That's the Taurean too, and it comes in real handy when trying to reach the top (of anything). And when the Taurean gets her beady little eyes on something, get out of the way, 'cause she's goin' after it and she's gonna get it. The word fear is not in their vocabulary, and they are indefatigable. Just try keeping up with one some night on a cruising spree of the local places.

When the bull-sign chooses his partner his wisest decision would be to settle on someone under the compatible signs of Virgo or Capricorn—the least compatible signs would be for them, Leo, Scorpio and Aquarius. Of course, these are only indications, but the natives of the first two mentioned signs are naturally sympathetic to Taurus, and helpful. They should make excellent partners in business or bed. But definite rules cannot be laid down, and the best thing to do is find out all you can about your own personality as indicated by the stars, then do the same thing for the "other person."

Those born between April 20th and April 30th—

Were born when the Sun was in the astrological sign of Taurus and Venus is their ruling planet. In general they possess the finer characteristics of the bull—quiet, easy-going—more-or-less inclined to do things their own way (and what's wrong with that?) and inclined equally to let others do things their own way, until aroused—and then, look out, world, here she comes; headstrong, unyielding and not giving a damn about the consequences.

The true Taurean child is known for his tremendous vitality, not only physical, but mental as well, and he is prone to enjoy both comfort and luxury. They seem to feel that all expenditures on creature comforts concerned with the home are the wisest of all. They do tend to express a large fondness for children, and in love are known to be both loyal and devoted, but are often so abstract as not to allow one to know the reality of their affections.

They are extremely imperturbable—so much so that

one seldom knows how deeply their feelings run, and this first part of the sign which comes under the special influence of the messenger of the gods, Mercury, is likely to produce an individual, with mind and heart, who is richly endowed—and we don't mind that, do we?

Venus and Mercury, both of which are ruling this part of the sign, tend to produce, or should we say induce (seduce in some cases) the natives into various pursuits. Mercury would tend to produce those children of Taurus who would be most interested in such occupations as manufacturing, farming, mining, building or something equally as practical. The combination of these influences may likely drive the native into less mundane professions.

Venus, being the ruling planet of the entire sign, would tend to lead its children into the professions favoring the arts, such as musicians, actors, florists, perfumers and couturiers, or anyone connected with the decorative arts or dealing with articles of adornment. Would you believe beads?

Mercury is different. I always did suspect that boy, after all, who wouldn't suspect someone who had wings on his feet, not to mention on his hat as well. Mercury would indicate success in endeavors of a literary nature, or booksellers, printers, teachers, accountants, interpreters, orators (they read the beads), registrars, clerks and letter carriers. These people, you see, are versatile, and that's what counts nowadays. All they have to do is make a selection from all these things, deciding, of course, on what is most congenial to them, then giving it all they've got.

They've got a campy line of flowers they can wear too; and colors. Daisies, cowslips, syringae, Narcissus, and trailing arbutus. Now there's a hell of a posie for you. Lemon-yellow, red-orange, slate, pale blue, and indigo are their best colors. Their stones; emerald, agate, topaz, marcasite, lapis-lazuli, coral, and beryl. It's not necessary that they wear these stones, colors, or flowers, however—but I don't really see how they could resist—but if they do they'll have the added satisfaction of knowing that they are dressing in harmony with the vibrations of their stars.

These people, above all, are ones who should let themselves go. They have been given warmth and affection by Taurus, and the power to attract by Venus. They should avoid, however, their tendency toward imperturbability from allowing them to show their love, and should temper their inclination toward persistency.

Those born between May 1st and May 9th—

Are influenced not only by the goddess of love, Venus, as are all Taureans, but also by that ruler of the senses, the Moon as well. Both of them are prominent in the heavens during these particular dates.

They have a lovely selection of flowers: violets, lilacs, narcissuses (or is it narcissi?), jonquils, daisies, cowslips and crane's-bills. Their stones: opals, moonstones, carnelians, corals and all stones that tend to be dull white and pale green. White (would you believe?), pale yellow, pale green, pale blue and lemon yellow are their colors. If they wear these colors, they are dressing in accord with their planetary vibrations, but it is not absolutely essential that they do so.

Taurus, being their sign, makes them naturally intensely practical. Building, mining and manufacturing are all pursuits which are in line with this, and in which the Taurean should succeed. However, with both the Moon and Venus working for them they might well be a little less practical and follow something in the field of journalism or entertainment. They might even combine the aspects and embark upon a career somewhat along the line of interior decoration.

No problems are foreseen for the Taurean in the field of love, especially with Venus working so hard for him. His only problem might lie in his expectancy that his affection is taken for granted. Not so! If he loves someone he must tell them about it, and it will be appreciated.

The dominant Venus in this sign also produces many jewelers, clothing designers, florists, perfumers, confectioners, etc. and is the principal planet to be taken into consideration when a choice of profession is made. Musicians, poets, painters, actors and all sorts of artists are favored by this configuration.

The children of this first third of Taurus will also come under the heavy influence of the Moon, and favors transportation, especially water transportation and all things connected with it such as international trade; not to mention all business connected with liquid. Salesmen (especially the traveling kind) are frequently born in this period, as well as other people who deal with the general public.

The line of business adopted by these Taureans is not so important since they have such a high degree of stick-to-it-iveness that makes success inevitable. They most often become so involved in business and other matters practical that they neglect the finer sides of their nature.

Healthwise they follow their symbol the bull, strong and sturdy. They might show a tendency to ailments of the throat such as laryngitis; tonsillitis or diphtheria. But with proper health habits, especially diet control and elimination they have no cause for worry at all.

They have an unusual equipment for success, but they must learn to use it properly. Sometimes it's necessary that they change their opinions (versatility counts) and the strong influence of the Moon in this part of the sign will aid them in that respect—if it is truly shown that they are approaching a problem from the wrong angle. Their penchant for hanging on to what they've got sometimes impedes their progress to bigger and better things. So swing, girl, swing!

Those born between May 10th and May 20th—

Are under a strong sign, one of the strongest of the Zodiac, Taurus the Bull. This is a sign which makes its children most tremendously vital as well as persistent, tenacious and practical. Unlike the Aries who leaves many things undone, once the Taurus child starts something he keeps working at it until it is finished. These characteristics under control and understood all tend to success.

They are affectionate and warm and exude a charm which has a great power to attract (and hold) partners. Their main trouble lies in the fact that they seldom express their feelings and expect to be taken for granted. They must learn to be demonstrative.

Generally speaking the Taurean tends to have a happy and harmonious domestic life, and works hard to achieve it. Nothing gives them greater satisfaction than to be surrounded by peace (piece?) and comfort in a home of their own. They are most agreeable and even-tempered until someone waves the red flag in front of their face, and when that happens you have the perfect example of the bull in the china shop. The crockery flies! Their passion goes to extremes in both directions, and they must exercise great will power to keep it in check.

Saturn is the ruler of this part of the sign of Taurus, and he is a strong ruler and a strict disciplinarian. His tendency is to make the native somewhat depressed, and the person so afflicted must make every effort not to let this effect control their life.

With all of their love of creature comforts the Taurean may have a tendency to overeat, and in order to maintain their health must learn to curb their appetite. This will go far to aiding their maintenance of physical strength to which they are heir. They should keep all of their natural functions in good operation with special care to the throat, but they have a finer side and should strive to develop the mental and spiritual as well.

At home or at work, if they can discard the depressing influence of Saturn which inflicts itself upon them from time to time there can be no doubt that they will succeed in these fields. The butch types can find happiness in mining, manufacturing, building, farming or almost anything else that is practical or constructive. The Saturnian aspect can lead to a certain amount of gravity in the selection of professions, even inducing certain individuals into the realms of sextons, undertakers and grave-diggers!

Venus, lover that she is, cannot be so easily dominated however, and will usually guide the native into less grave professions, perhaps more inspiring ones, ones more suited, as it were, to the less butch, such as music, poetry, art, theater; they may even become manufacturer's of women's clothing, or possibly will have a great deal to do with articles of adornment or good things to eat. The Taurean is both talented and creative and has a wide choice of fields open to him.

Being so arty it only follows that he should be surrounded by gay colors, flowers and jewels. The colors that are in harmony with his nature are: pale blue, indigo, lemon-yellow, black, dark brown (uh-huh) and lead gray; flowers; trailing arbutus, violet (but definitely not shrinking), hyacinth, daisy (no comment), cowslip and jonquil; jewels; lodestone, moonstone, opal, beryl, carnelian, sapphire and chrysolite. If the native should choose not to wear them because they are unbecoming it would be of little import, but these are the ones in harmony with the time of his birth.

Imperturbability is the keyword of these children of Taurus, and Venus lends them a most influential charm. Strength of the bull and the high ideals of Saturn combine to enable them to realize their high, although materialistic ideals. Industry conquers all.

CHAPTER THREE
GEMINI

MAY 21ST THROUGH JUNE 21ST

Twins have constantly provided an enigma for all people who ever come in contact with them. First there is the problem of how to tell them apart. And then, they seem to have such perverse natures, taking an enormous amount of pleasure in confusing people with their very alikeness.

In the local cruising places, with minds already slightly befuddled by high spirits and alcoholic ones, they can create even greater confusion, and frequently do. At the same time, as one gets to know them, differences between them are observed. Yet the veneer of likeness works in their behalf. Inexplicable, enigmatic and unpredictable are the adjectives that probably best describe twins.

Gemini presents much the same problem to the astrologer. The sign is elusive, yet interesting—but basically complex. Reviewing the first three signs of the Zodiac, one says that Aries is idealistic, Taurus is dependable, but Gemini is a question mark, predictably unpredictable. Aries is a fire sign, and its children, fiery; Taurus is an earth sign, and its children, earthly.

Gemini is an air sign, and its children are most definitely airy. Not only because the sign belongs to what is called the air triplicity of Gemini, Libra, and Aquarius, but especially so, since it is ruled by the planet of the messenger of the gods, Mercury with his winged feet and winged helmet. Quick of motion, in all directions, the Gemini person moves constantly, up and down, side to side, and back and forth.

Mercury lends to these people all of the high intellectual qualities that it stands for, and cannot be considered an unfortunate influence, but the twins are powerful and tend to dissipate the mental powers of the native when they start to pull in their opposite directions. The Gemini person, then, must concentrate on bringing together all of these high mental qualities, and struggle to keep together those strengths which would be disorganized by his own sign.

Their Mercury also gives them versatility, volatility and facility; diplomacy, tactfulness and suavity; along with vision, intuition and understanding. It would seem that with all these noble qualities that nothing could go wrong with the native, but unfortunately, Gemini is often his own worst enemy. He must give both of his twins something to do to keep them occupied, or frequently the one will destroy what the other has done. Mentally he has twice as much energy as most people, and can do twice as much, and thereby travel two roads at the same time toward a common goal.

Those who are in the workaday world will most likely choose a profession that requires a great deal of mental dexterity and will use all of his mental forces during business hours to that end—then as an avocation will select a pursuit, perhaps of another variety that will not only keep the balance of his mind active, but will further him along the way to his goal, perhaps by improving his ability to accomplish his regular work.

The Gemini homemaker has the ability to take the drudgery out of housework (she hates it) not by avoiding it, but by seeing and putting to use new ways of doing things. They are most efficient planners and managers. And they strive to get menial tasks out of the way quickly so that they may follow their inclinations to more intellectual pursuits—perhaps pursuits that will make them more interesting companions or more successful as mates.

The Gemini is going to have two lines of action anyway, and it is just as well, since he will scatter his forces, that he should scatter them according to a plan. And a well thought-out and followed plan will not only work out better for them, but also for those around them. Oh, Gemini is the sign of the lungs especially, but also all dual organs...imagine, dual organs!

Astrology teaches us too that the fall of the Gemini is all too often their failure to concentrate. They can do things more easily, they can do things more gracefully, they can do things more successfully than can most people—and perhaps because of this natural ease, grace and success they become bored and often do nothing at all. They lack the driving force of the Aries children to goad them to the heights; they lack the sense of responsibility of the Taurean which leads him one-foot-after-the-other to his goal. They must cultivate deliberation and determination in order to achieve the realization of their capacities.

Failure to concentrate in business is only one phase in which the Gemini may be adversely affected. In the realm of romance this same failure can prove equally disastrous. They are born flirts, often philanderers, and this scattering of attention can often lose them the affections of the person whom they really and truly love. If they are not yet settled down to one person, they frequently carry on a number of affairs at the same time (and sometimes with a high degree of success).

When (and if) the Gemini does determine to settle down, he will find the most likely partners born under the signs of either Libra or Aquarius. Those signs least likely to make a match with him would be Virgo, Saggitarius and Pisces. Of course, these are only indi-cations—but the natives of the first two mentioned signs are naturally sympathetic to Gemini, and helpful. They should make excellent partners in business or bed. But definite rules cannot be laid down, and the best thing to do is find out all one can about one's own personality as indicated by the stars, then do the same for the "other person"...or persons—Geminis are natu-rals for what polite society calls the "ménage à trois."

Those born between May 21st and May 31st—

Were born under the sign which rules the United States. (The Declaration of Independence was signed when Gemini was rising. We haven't discussed rising signs, and probably won't in this basic guide.) And they possess that most American characteristic, versatility (and a mighty important characteristic, I might add). BUT, this is their strength AND their weakness.

The highly intellectual Mercury dominates and rules the sign, and gives his subjects an extremely sensitive and highly developed mentality. They are able to see both sides of a subject, but must learn to decide for themselves and not to be easily swerved by the opinions of others.

The Gemini person is under a sign whose symbol is a pair of twins, and each must have its pursuit. The native of the sign can best resolve his tendency to scatter his forces by giving each side of his nature something to do, and doing them both at the same time if possible—or at least alternately, and tiring of one, turn to the other. Such activity remedies his tendency to stray from accomplishment and satisfies his perpetual desire for change (or you might consider it a desire for perpetual change). Success for the Gemini almost always depends upon his following two roads simultaneously toward the same goal.

Their memories border on the photographic as well as the phonographic (thought I said something else, didn't you?)—and be careful what you say or do in their presence. They see, even when they don't appear to be looking. These gifts, wisely used and combined with concentration and will power form the best vehicle for the road to success.

They tend to be nervous people and should be careful of their nerves. They should exercise and sleep more than most people and strive to attain and maintain an air and attitude of both mental and physical calmness in order to avoid the ailments of neuritis and rheumatic difficulties which may strike at their nerve centers.

The dominant planet in this segment of Gemini is Jupiter, and jovial Jove tends to give his children a generous disposition. This planet also gives an ability to rise to great heights and a feeling for humanity in general. Those most influenced by Jupiter are likely to find themselves engaged in judicial, literary or artistic pursuits.

Literary occupations are especially indicated by Mercury, the ruler of this sign, and he leads his children often into careers as writers, editors, publishers, printers and booksellers. Sometimes though the Mercurial individual will be led into education, accountancy or linguistics; or perhaps he will be a registrar or a clerk.

Jupiter, the truly beneficent planet, favors no particular line of endeavor; and though he leads those closest to him into such fields as law, banking, religion, etc., he smiles equally upon whatever particular field the native may choose.

If dressing in harmony with their stars is of particular importance to the individual under this sign, he may choose from the following flowers: lily-of-the-valley, myrtle, mayflower and bittersweet; the following jewels: beryl, emerald, sapphire, agate, topaz and marcasite; and the following colors: orange, yellow, slate, purple (royal, of course) and violet (some call it lavender).

Facile, easy-come-easy-go, Gemini. They love beauty, everywhere, and simply adore 'atmosphere.' Candlelight and wine, gypsy violins, sweet nothings, ah! Their homes are invariably charming (one man after another; they're delightful flirts) and once they can control that latter, they'll make some man a delightful husband.

Those born between June 1st and June 9th—

Were born when the Sun was in Gemini, the sign of the twins. And the intellectual Mercury rules the sign.

This combination produces almost invariably a versatile mentality which is highly sensitive, capable of reaching great heights, yet subject to falls from these heights. Their thirst for knowledge is almost insatiable—and once learned they can't wait to apply it in a new (and sometimes devious) way. They're enjoyment comes from 'doing' though, and not from the outcome particularly. What do you think of that?

So we have Gemini, the Sun and Mercury working on them, and in this particular realm of the heavens we add a touch of Mars. Now he does give strength, courage and energy to his subjects—all of which make for success; but he also adds a tendency toward over-aggressiveness, quarrelsomeness and (shades of S&M) violence. It's best that the Gemini not let these latter dominate his character.

Concentration is the best if not the only answer to counteracting these latter Martian influences. Two outlets for their mental activities are most important. Their desire for change must, simply must, be satisfied, and the tendency for them is if they don't find it in one field, they'll find it in another. By concentration on two parallel outlets one goal can be accomplished without the sacrifice of those already accomplished in other realms.

The colors for those born at this time are blood-red, green, blue, yellow, slate, and appropriately for many, scarlet. Their flowers are myrtle, bittersweet, which name describes their double nature, lily-of-the-valley, and mayflower. Moon crystal, beryl, agate, emerald, and topaz are their jewels. If they decide to dress in harmony with their stars they will wear these jewels, flowers and colors, at least to love-ins and drag balls, but if they should find them unbecoming to them, it is not necessary that they do so.

Gemini can be quite successful in their relationships with friends, sisters and others as long as they don't become too contentious with them. The children with a Martian influence frequently tend to picking fights. Petty strife, however, does not become them. They should learn to be lovers and not fighters and use the Mars influence to add strength to their character, and in turn, charm.

They also tend to try to do so many things at one time that sometimes they find it difficult to concentrate on the one they love. Such actions could pave the road to Reno. They are, after all, only one person in spite of the fact that their sign is symbolized by twins—and shouldn't try to spread it around like they were.

Geminis should also get plenty of time in bed—resting. Their nerves are their most delicate condition and they can seldom sit still. It would behoove them as well to get sufficient exercise, fresh air and eat a proper balanced diet. Then to add to their strength they might cultivate a certain amount of mental and physical poise.

If the native of Gemini can learn to command himself, he will be capable of assuming a position of commanding and would most likely succeed as a lawyer, banker or diplomat. Their natural ability toward effective public speaking will help them a great deal in this regard.

Mercury rules the intellect and the sign of Gemini, and its benevolent influence will be felt in almost any line of endeavor, and especially favors writers, editors, publishers, printers and booksellers. Teachers, accountants, orators, registrars and clerks also come under this influence.

Their choice of profession has a secondary influence from the planet Mars—and though it might not lead one into a Martian profession, it will aid the native in any profession where courage, initiative and aggressiveness and executive ability come into play. Profession-wise, though, Mars favors soldiers, surgeons, chemists, dentists, barbers, iron and steel dealers and all those who work with sharp instruments—including the tongue.

Arguing and bickering seldom, if ever, are of any avail to the Gemini person. They should avoid discussions. Charm is their most persuasive attribute.

Those born between June 10th and June 21st—

Are probably the most favored in the sign of Gemini. They are by the nature of the sign airy and intellectual, and in addition, they come under the influence of the Sun, the ruler of honor, fame and advancement in life, since it rules this particular segment of Gemini.

Successful brokers, bankers, lawyers and diplomats, aided by their knack for public oratory, are often Gemini-born. If any of these lines are to their liking the Gemini will no doubt succeed in his efforts, but they have the Sun ruling their part of this sign and, of course, the heavy influence of the sign's ruler, Mercury, and will probably seek a profession that will somehow deal with literature, art or science.

Public officials have the Sun in their favor, as do those who would follow a profession of working with precious metals and jewelers. The chief factor in determining a profession, however, is Mercury, the intellectual, and he will usually lead his children into more literary pursuits and many of them will become writers, printers, publishers, editors and booksellers. Some may be lead into the fields of accountancy, interpreting, teaching and clerking.

Perhaps they may choose none of these indicated professions, but in any case they've got the benevolent influences of both the Sun and Mercury swinging for them as dominant planets and derive strength from the Sun and high intellect from Mercury.

The jewels indicated for these Geminis are topaz, emerald, beryl, and chrysolite; and their flowers are mayflower, myrtle, bittersweet, and lily-of-the-valley. Their colors are orange, slate, yellow-brown, and gold. They can if they wish incorporate any or all of these into their dress (although it might look rather tacky, all of these at once), or if they feel that the indications are not becoming to them, they are free not to wear them.

They possess the characteristic versatility of their sign of the twins, Gemini, but can easily exaggerate this blessing into the curse of changeableness.

Gemini persons are usually generously equipped— with nerves and sometimes other things. This is generally the rule among those who have the characteristic of versatility along with a highly developed mentality and a nature that is over-sensitive. They are prone to rheumatic and neuritic pains in the arms especially. Proper diet, combined with sufficient exercise, rest and fresh air (it would be best though if they didn't get this while cruising the parks in some larger metropolitan centers) are the best regimens to follow to avoid these conditions.

It is possible that they may not amass a great deal of wealth materially speaking—but frequently the Gemini puts more importance on a work itself than he does on the compensation for that work. Being nervous, he goes through many periods of restlessness and anxiety. He is tempted to try many things and once having established his best course, he is able to sail right on through to fame and success.

CHAPTER FOUR
CANCER

JUNE 22ND THROUGH JULY 21ST

Cancer introduces us to the first sign in what is called the water triplicity. The Aries people were fiery, the Taureans were earthy, and the Geminis, airy. But even though Cancer is a water sign, you won't find that they are wishy-washy. Their ruling planet is the Moon, and frequently they are referred to nowadays as Moon Children.

Their symbol is the crab—and in a way they are crab-like. You know how they get hold and won't let go. Well, the people born between these dates certainly have that capacity in common with crabs. Tenaciousness is one of the qualities of this sign for which it is best known. And, they sometimes go at things sidewise rather than head-on.

The nature of the Cancer is a loyal one. There are many fixed loyalties to which he adheres and the typical Moon Child is a traditionalist and clings to established precedents, customs and habits. He is loyal to and loves his home and extends this fidelity to his family, his neighborhood and his community. This applies, however, as it does to his choice of mate. These are placed affections and loyalties. He may be slow in placing his love, but once it is fixed, it certainly is not like the ever-changing moon nor indicated by the watery nature of the sign.

But in spite of all this constant love and devotion to their home, they have a wanderlust that is unbelievable. The Moon urges them on to new and strange vistas constantly, and they love travel in foreign lands—and are especially attracted to sea-coasts.

The Moon Child is drawn by water, and by those things which deal with water. They make great sailors (and sometimes small and middle size ones too) and explorers; yet in most cases where they have pursued these vocations they eventually conquer their lust for meandering and return to their native land. Their love of the traditional and loyalty which is ingrained in them nearly always brings them back to their home port.

As you can see these two inclinations, the love of home and the love of travel could and does have a profound effect upon the native. Their methods of thought and action tend to make the Cancerian a rather moody person. The highly developed Cancerian will conquer this conflict and be the master of his moods; the ones that are not successful in this become slaves to their moods.

The feminine Moon which rules Cancer will generally endow the native with an almost feminine sensitivity. This trait is secondary only to their characteristic of tenacity, and can enable them to make themselves very adaptable, thereby harvesting the best of life out of all that is around them—but, on the other hand, he may look too deeply inside himself, become overly self-analytic, driving himself into a shell of his own creation.

It is of course best for the native, and for those around him to develop the first of these alternatives. They can become successful in lines such as preaching, teaching and oratory as have many famous Moon Children.

In dealing with the Cancer person, their associates, friends, and even lovers should take into consideration this trait of sensitivity. They become resentful if pushed too hard, and sympathy and understanding are necessary when relating to them.

They are born lovers, and you couldn't want anyone more romantic or imaginative. Sensitive and loyal people, they take great delight in exploring all the nuances and delights of love. They are frequently very proud persons, too much so sometimes to show their feelings to others. They tend to be shy and go out of their way to avoid ridicule or repulse. Frequently this combination of traits leads them into misunderstandings with those near and dear to them and in such a milieu you wouldn't believe. They hardly deserve it and can be only vaguely aware of the causes.

Their tenacity and patience are their saving graces and they can and most often will hold out until the right thing comes along. They might face a sea of troubles, but come through and break down the often self-imposed barriers between them and their love. Then, if the object of their affections is worthy, the ensuing relationship will be both richly satisfying and lasting.

When the Moon Child chooses his partner his wisest decision would be to settle on someone under the compatible signs of Scorpio or Pisces—the least compatible signs would be for them, Libra, Capricorn and Aries. Of course, these are only indications—but the natives of the first two mentioned signs are naturally sympathetic to Cancer, and helpful. They should make excellent partners in business or in bed. But definite rules cannot be laid down, and the best thing to do is find out all one can about one's own personality as indicated by the stars, then do the same thing for the "other person."

The Cancerian is frequently very psychic and many mediums have been born under the influences of this sign. It has been said that they clearly see the past and the future, just as clearly as the present. The downfall of some might be their tendency to almost live in the past, but their sensitivity clearly to see the future tends to draw them out of this, and their ability to foresee the future hinges a great deal upon their study of the past. They are seldom revolutionists, more often being reformers. He frequently is a leader but never of a new movement whose course might be unknown, and tends to walk sideways to his goal.

Physically speaking the sign of Cancer rules the stomach, and this is an important influence on the entire being of the Moon Child. Frequently in the

Cancer home the dining room is the most lavish room of all, and the Cancerian male can make a nuisance of himself in the kitchen. They tend to over accentuate the part that eating plays in the social scheme of things; and being water signed persons under the rulership of the Moon they put an exaggerated value on the part of liquids at times too. The Moon Child would do well to note that eating and drinking can be hazardous to the health as well as a ladder to success.

The most serious problem of the Cancerian, though, is his tendency to worry. Nearly all of his aches, pains and ailments can be traced to mental or emotional causes. They fuss and fume over their loved ones till they make themselves ill, then start all over again to fuss and fume over themselves. And the spiral can continue viciously—so Cancerians, beware. They are not by nature strong people. The Moon is not as strong as the Sun, as robust as Jupiter or as vigorous as Mars. Nor is the Cancerian really weak—and by exercising proper mental habits and reasonable physical care they can control their bodies.

Patience is for these people a saving quality against their tendencies toward fretfulness, sensitivity and bitterness. They suffer and endure—but patience is the quality they have that should be used in their suffering and enduring.

Those born between June 22nd and July 1st—

Have as their ruling planets the Moon and Venus. The Moon naturally governs the home, the Mother, travels and marital (or pre- or extra-marital) affairs.

Love and art are under the domination of Venus. Social pleasures and enjoyment come heavily under the influence of the love goddess, who also figures prominently in all to do with jewels, clothes and to some extent, money.

It is strange that in this configuration we can see a most complex individual. We have the changeable Moon and the loving and colorful Venus both modified by the conservative Cancer. The person possessing all of these traits, you can see, would have a rather paradoxical, if not enigmatic nature.

The colors for these people tend to run to the cool and watery, and are light blue, violet, silver, white, lemon-yellow, pale green and pale blue. Their flowers are moonflower (very appropriate), wallflower (difficult to pick; one foot seems rooted to the wall); and their jewels are opal, moonstone, crystal and other dull white and pale green stones. If these Cancerians choose to wear these jewels, colors and flowers they will be dressing in harmony with their stars. Their basic conservatism may make them very self conscious about this though, and if they feel that they are unbecoming to them, Moon Children will wisely avoid such adornment.

The native will tend to be very affectionate and protective to his lover. He's not coquettish or flirtatious like the natives of Gemini and Libra. They are constant when finally in love, and chaste! They really enjoy good things to eat, and can provide the same for others—it is truly said, and they know it, one of the way to a man's heart is through his stomach.

Changeability and recklessness characterize the Venus influenced Moon Child, but these traits are only superficial, and underneath they have a tendency to tenacity that is most laudable and which should be cultivated. In addition to their feelings of protectiveness and affection toward their loved ones, they have a capacity to be self-sacrificing and long-suffering.

They have a strong feeling for tradition and heritage, and enjoy such expressions of them as pedigrees and heirlooms. They like their homes, but they like to travel as well, and will frequently be led to new adventures, especially if it is near or concerns the sea.

The Moon Children have a natural gift for all things dealing with liquid, or water transportation—shipping enterprises, import and export; and also for those enterprises dealing in some way with the mixing of fluids with other ingredients, such as chemistry, or activities dealing with foods.

Venus supplements this latter and would tend to make her children proficient as confectioners, bakers and pastry chefs. The love goddess supplementing the action of the Moon again would aid the native to enter the fields of perfumery or clothing design. Their talents might also lie in the realm of music, poetry, painting, acting or any other artistic endeavor, and if they have such a talent, they should develop it if only as an avocation.

The Moon's influence is stronger though and is the ruler of the sign of Cancer, and will most likely be the determining factor in the selecting of an occupational field. It governs sailors (mmmh!), exporters and importers, shipping merchants, travelers and all transportation, but especially water, and those engaged with liquids.

However, this tendency toward liquids could also lead to an over fascination with the consumption of alcohol. This is a pleasure which should not be carried too far—it's nice to know what you go home with. Digestion and gastric disturbances can be a problem for these people too. Simple living would be best for them, but it is difficult for them to achieve. And one last word for them—careful of your throat!

Those born between July 2nd and July 11th—

Were also born under the Zodiacal sign of the Crab, Cancer, and are Children of the Moon. Both the symbol and the name of the sign sound very disagreeable, but their influences, fortunately are not so much so.

Position-wise, people born between these dates can rise to great heights of prominence. John D. Rockefeller and Calvin Coolidge are both Cancerians, and men worthy of such profound respect as these can hardly be said to have been born under unlucky stars.

Cancer, you see then, is a most fortunate sign, and consequently, so are those people born under its influences. And this part of the sign, falling as it does under the secondary rulership of the intellectual Mercury is the most fortunate part of the sign. Such a combination is almost undefeatable in traveling the highway to fortune and fame.

By their associations and friends these Cancerians are often unjustly considered to be fickle. Thin-skinned, overly sensitive and suffering from imagined slights they may be, but they are exceedingly loyal and in the case of the one (and unlike many of their sisters, it is one) they love, they frequently make great self-sacrifices. In their devotion toward the object of their affection they are often patronizing and paternal. They are extremely romantic, but their domesticity is their greater love.

Their colors run a gamut of shades. They are white, pale yellow, pale green, violet, silver, blue and black. Their flowers are the moonflower and the wallflower (and they're frequently successful in rooting one from its location). Jewelwise they should find marcasite, agate, topaz, emerald, opal, moonstone and crystal planetarily compatible. There is no reason at all that they have to wear these stones, colors or flowers, should they find them at all unbecoming—but if they do wear them they are in harmony with the music of their spheres.

Asthma frequently attacks these natives, and they should guard against over-taxing their vocal cords. Self-indulgences can be a pitfall to them as well, particularly over-eating and immoderate consumption of alcohol.

They will be drawn to occupations dealing with liquids by the influence of their ruling planet, the Moon. They will be led to be (or do) sailors, shipping merchants, travelers, fishermen and those engaged in transportation, especially water transportation.

The Mercurial influence will no doubt give them some bent along the lines of more intellectual pursuits or the production of literature. Mercury's children are frequently writers, printers, booksellers, editors and publishers—and in combination with the Moon will frequently produce accountants, clerks, salesmen, teachers, interpreters and letter carriers. Their field is wide, and wisely followed can lead them onto the road to success.

Oversensitivity is really the only trait that might lead them off the path to fame in whatever field they choose. It could make enemies out of an acquaintance or business associates who lacked understanding, and cause temporary discord or embarrassment between friends. Their fullest development relies upon harmony.

Above all they should not be afraid to try the new, and should have confidence in themselves that they are able to succeed.

Those born between July 12th and July 21st—

Were born most heavily under the influence of Cancer, and as such seem to be most decidedly determined on experiencing the entire range of human sensations.

The Moon, their ruling planet, is doubly powerful

between these dates, and those born under its influences will be especially attracted to travel, adventure
and to the occult sciences. Conditions in their life
will undoubtedly be constantly changing, and they
may even attain a certain amount of public acclaim or
recognition and might even acquire property, without
even trying to do so.

Even so, the symbol of their sign is the crab, and
this means that the native would more than likely tend
to be conservative, and would cling to tradition and
think twice before estranging himself from familiar
stomping grounds. It's difficult to say what persons
might do with these two opposing influences. Much
would depend upon their individual, complete horoscope. In the case of the typical Moon Child, however,
their conservative nature is the one that finally wins
out.

The planetary influences indicate that their best
colors would be violet, pale yellow, pale green, silver
and white; and that their flowers are moonflower and
the wallflower (they like them, they aren't them). Their
jewels are indicated to be nearly all of the dull white
and pale green stones, including opal, moonstone and
crystal. If these are all to their liking and they choose
to adorn themselves with them they are dressing with
their stars.

It is not necessary, however, that they do, and if they
decide that these jewels, colors and flowers are unbecoming to them, and not to wear them, it is of little
consequence.

The most notable lack in these children of Cancer is that of self-confidence. They tend to cling to the past and all of its traditions. There's nothing intrinsically wrong with this sentimentality, except that in the case of these persons it becomes an obstacle on their road to success. They must, somehow, attain self-confidence in order to get ahead.

As the Moon is dependent upon the Sun for its light, these persons are dependent frequently upon their friends. But the Moon also tends to make her children of a sensitive nature and they frequently take offense at imagined slights. Hyper-sensitivity and a tendency to confuse visions of the future with remembrances of things past are two gifts of the Moon that test the mettle of the Cancer born.

Shipping, importing and exporting and related lines may appeal to these people because of their great interest in travel. Their inclination toward the kitchen might lead them to follow dietetic and chemical pursuits. They do love children, and can be quite successful in almost any activity where the raising and handling of the young is involved.

The dominant planet in their chart is the Moon, which governs sailors, shipping merchants, importers and dealers in liquids, salesmen and others dealing with the public (hustlers?). They'll seldom go wrong if they follow any of these.

As the Moon is the queen of the skies, and the ruler of their sign, they tend to want to live like queens, and wine and dine like them as well. But, their stomach is one of their weakest points (watch them gulp the Rolaids) and they should guard against immoderate intake. Asthma and related upper respiratory ailments tend to attack them from time to time as well. But if they learn to eat a little lower on the hog, they'll survive to a ripe, and happy, old age.

CHAPTER FIVE
LEO

JULY 22ND THROUGH AUGUST 21ST

Leo is symbolized astrologically by the lion, king of the beasts. And, as the lion figures prominently in many royal crests, Leo is also the royal sign.

The most typical natives of the sign of Leo are masterful, high-minded types and have a great deal of executive ability. This ability is exercised in both their business and social lives. (Just watch one of them holding court!) They are the queens of the circle to which they belong. They were born to rule and they see to it that they do. However, they must learn to rule themselves as well and keep their desire for authority in check, else they may tend to be authoritative and domineering.

People are drawn to them by their magnetic personalities, and the Leo should always strive for personal interviews if he is going to make a point with a person. They intensely like underhandedness and double-dealing. They are filled with ambition, industry, and are virtually tireless, but they dislike the menial tasks that may become necessary from time to time. They become unhappy and discontented when their ambitions are thwarted, and although it does them some good from time to time to be so discontented, they should not let it rule their lives.

The bulk of their strength is derived from their ruling planet, the Sun. This heavenly body governs, in the physical body notably the heart, the back and the arteries, and those born under the Zodiacal sign of Leo should be on the watch for any symptoms appearing in those regions of the body. Seldom are they afflicted by ailments that are functional in nature and therefore they should pay particular attention to those things which might be symptomatic of diseases of a more organic nature. This is especially true if they suffer from dizzy spells, poor eyesight, or anything that would indicate a disorder of the heart or arterial system.

Their natural executive ability is indicated by their sign. If at all possible they should be connected with the executive division of the business with which they are associated, if not at the head of the business itself. They fit quite well, and naturally into any situation in which they can be queen bee, and are excellent in the positions of managers, superintendents, sales managers, directors and corporation officers.

Their natural high-mindedness makes them, fortunately, inclined to use their talents for the good of all. They are most deserving of the mark of royalty, inasmuch as they do possess a rare executive ability, are untiring workers and of a generous and forgiving nature. *Noblesse oblige* is one of their most highly developed senses.

In marriage, as well as in all phases of his life the Leo born wishes to dominate, and his natural magnetism and personality usually gain him that position of dominance. And the person so attached to the Leo would do well to let him dominate since love is the natural realm for him.

The fiery Aries-born and the open frank Sagittarius people are generally considered to be the best matches for the Leo people. The position of the Sun in their horoscopes most definitely indicates a great deal of congeniality in such a relationship. But matrimony is a very personal matter, and a scientific astrologer would insist upon having not only the month of a person's birth, but the day, year, hour and place as well before advising a person in this wise. And of course, it would be impossible for him to tell the result of such a match unless the same information were available concerning the prospective "other half." Two charts should harmonize in order to assure that two people would harmonize. Then, again, generally speaking, the least compatible mates for the lion would be those born under the signs of Scorpio, Aquarius and Taurus.

The energies of the Leo are all too often dissipated on efforts that might as well be handled by others, and the Leo should leave the non-essentials to these other people. They must learn to conquer their desire to rule in everything. They do not need to be the dominating force all the time. They'll get the really important things in life as a result of their inherent abilities and magnetic personalities.

Leo people also have a great hunger for applause and sometimes this leads them onto the stage. But more often it develops only into a tendency to show off. Leos are good people and they know it. They have no need to impress other people with their ability or their goodness. It sticks out all over them. They do have authoritative ability and can rule, if they so choose, without appearing to. The latter would be their wiser course.

The Leo is prone to open retaliation when vexed or angered. He is hardly likely to resort to subterfuge or underhanded retribution. Blessed with natural charm and manners they frequently get their own way without half trying. Sometimes their personal magnetism, which gains them so many friends and admirers, invites the envy or jealousy of others to be directed toward them.

Regimentation is a dirty word to the Leo and he has no patience with "chain of command." He wants to deal direct. They don't readily realize that the largest of enterprises move exceeding slow, not by leaps and bounds; and he has to hold his impatience in check and move and progress slowly in order to realize his goals.

They have a grand destiny and it is important that they realize their shortcomings and avoid them if they would develop to their fullest. They are capable, strong and forceful, able to lead and direct and should do so. They should strive to be adventurous and not shrink from hazardous undertakings, and success should be theirs anywhere under the Sun (or son).

Those who do not make complete use of the gifts the stars have granted them, have not lived up to their royal sign.

Those born between July 22nd and August 2nd—

Were born of course in the sign of Leo, symbolized by the Lion. Leo is ruled by the Sun, and is considered the royal sign of the Zodiac. Queenly, in a word.

The Sun completely rules only one sign, and that sign is Leo. Leo people are very lion-like in that they are inherently masterful, yet this masterfulness is tempered by a gentility and kindliness, which can only be ascribed to the finer vibrations emanating from the Sun and playing upon the extra-consciousness of the native. Impetuous and impulsive, those born under this sign become very passionate when their affections are involved. Two of their most characteristic traits are loyalty and constancy.

Those born under the sign of Leo have a natural intuition, but they are also impulsive, which makes it necessary for them to be very careful and distinguish between impulse and intuition. In making important decisions and in replying to letters that may be unpleasant they should, before taking action, reflect calmly. Their intuition, however, is usually very good, and they should beware of letting their judgment get in the way of it and go contrariwise, especially in their dealings with other people. Sometimes they appear to be boastful, dictatorial and overly ambitious as a result of their self-confidence and determined will.

The planet of discipline, Saturn, fortunately for the natives of this portion of Leo dominant at the time when they were born, and since these people have been endowed with very strong qualities as mentioned, they are in need of this discipline. However, this same aspect requires that they be constantly on their guard against false pride, self-deception, hazardous speculations and domestic discord. There are times when they should not assert themselves.

They have been given a great vitality because of their ruling planet the Sun, the giver of life, and are able to fight off many of the common afflictions that attack most people. On the other hand they must avoid fits of temper and the physical exertion to which they are prone. These could have a serious effect on their weaker physical parts, namely the heart and the back. The best counsel that could be given them is to live sensibly.

The basic love nature (and I ask you, how basic is basic?) is also ruled by Leo. They are very dependent upon affection, and must have an outlet for their emotions. They are often accused of having exaggerated egos and being exhibitionists; all of which is a result of their desire for approval and praise. "Speak softly but carry a big stick—" (every pun intended) would be their best motto. Of course, the stick doesn't have to be big if they know how to wield it. Heartbreak and sorrow may from time to time afflict them, and they must learn to rise above it, else it may eventually develop into a real physical ailment. For the same reason they should strive to control their tendencies to give way to fits of temper and over-exertion.

When they are out to get their man they too frequently want to show off. Saturn will aid them in guarding against this mistake in most cases. And in trapping their man they must also guard against seeming too masterful, dictatorial or overbearing; depending, of course on the situation. There are times when being masterful is the thing to do, but some situations call for the other side of Leo to predominate, namely that side which is warm and affectionate. In other words, pet, don't be *too* butch.

The planetary colors to which they vibrate are yellow, orange, lead-gray and black, and their flowers are the marigold and the peony. Their jewels are diamonds (and girl's best friend), rubies, lodestones, topaz and all gems that are dark in color and unpolished. If they wear these stones, flowers and colors they are dressing in harmony with their stars, but it is of no consequence, should they, upon deciding that these are unbecoming to them, decide not to wear them.

The Sun is the strongest influence in their choice of a profession since it is the ruling planet of their sign, and smiles favorably on those in high places, especially those involved in statesmanship and commerce.

Saturn is of course the secondary influence and directs them into less glamorous fields as mining, real estate, coal and wood business—and all businesses dealing with lead products like plumbing; generally speaking into all endeavors requiring perspiration and a strong back. I don't think I'll go into some of the jobs I've worked that called for those qualities.

They should also do well in all fields dealing with precious metals, especially jewelry making.

Their field is wide, and therefore, all that is necessary is for them to find a niche congenial to them.

Those born between August 3rd and August 13th—

Have about the best stars of all swinging for them, and upon which they can swing. The greater fortune, Jupiter, was dominant at the time of their birth, and to top it off they were born under the royal sign of Leo the lion and are also under the sign of the giver of life, the Sun.

Very sociable, indeed, they make friends easily and are great favorites at a party because of the charming personalities. Warm-hearted and lovable, they are ready to go to the rescue of anyone who is near and dear to them, and take as a personal injury any criticism of their close friends and associates.

Oftentimes their greatest weakness is their want of compliments and attention, and their ability to accept criticism is lessened by their great sensitiveness. Their greatest happiness comes frequently through making others happy, and the Sun seems to perpetuate in their spirit a feeling of youth, and even though they advance in years they continue to attract as friends very young people, which in turn helps to keep them both active and young themselves.

They have the generous high-mindedness characteristic of the sign of Leo along with the disdain for anything petty or underhanded, and are indeed, probably the most fortunate of Leos, inasmuch as they also have the benevolent Jupiter strong in their charts which makes them kind, generous, sympathetic and humane as well.

Their colors are sea-green, blue, purple (royal, naturally), yellow, violet and mixtures of red and indigo. Their flowers are the marigold and the peony, and their jewels the amethyst, the emerald, the diamond, the ruby and the sapphire. If their tendency to show off holds true they might tend to try to wear all of these at the same time, but if their sense tells them better, or if they find these unbecoming, it is of no import should they decide not to wear them.

The Leo queen in her castle is constantly holding court. The entire domestic circle is centered in its titular head, if that head is a Leo. They expect it and make sure of it, and they rule it. And they succeed, not only by their own worth, in almost anything they undertake, but also through inheritance, marriage and through fortunate speculations.

Many sales managers are found born under the sign of Leo, and they are peculiarly capable in this regard, combining, as they do their talents for managerial ability and salesmanship. They are capable even of the management of great enterprises as a result of their natural executive ability and their reputations for tireless application to work. Many Leos are found as presidents and managers of large corporations, and they are well-suited for these positions by their forcefulness and their natural desire to dominate.

The most influential factor in directing their choice of profession is their ruling planet, the Sun. It especially favors its children entering into statesmanship or commerce, and all those in high positions. It lends its support too to all those working precious metals and to jewelers in particular.

The "middle" Leos are most highly favored in having a secondary planet in Jupiter who almost guarantees success in every endeavor (even cruising).

As an occupation, though, he favors lawyers, judges, clergymen, physicians and bankers—all important people. The chief of the gods also takes an interest in tailors, provisioners, and all people engaged in selling good things to eat or wear.

The Leo-born are well equipped to succeed in many fields. Their masterfulness and natural executive ability almost guarantees it to them. They would do well to heed the reflection of Macbeth when he says:

> "I have no spur
> To prick the sides of my intent, but only
> Vaulting ambition, which o'erleaps itself
> And falls on the other."

Those born between August 14th and August 21st—

Find that responsibility lies heavily upon them. They were born in the third decant of the sign of the lion, Leo, whose dominant planet is the Sun. The third decant has as its secondary ruler the god of war Mars, which was dominant in the heavens at the time of their birth.

They tend to be somewhat boastful concerning their friends, their family and their belongings, and their own achievements; in spite of the fact that their Leo nature makes them warm-hearted, overly generous and sympathetic. Anything that they possess automatically becomes the best in the world, at least in their eyes. They do not like to be "second best," and strive to win or be first in games and contests, and in the eyes of their associates. Good judgment is necessary to overcome this trait which could easily become a stumbling block to them, inasmuch as those around them may well resent their superior airs and show-off tendencies.

Blowing their own horn is not necessary for them (if they could do it, even), and the Mars predominant in their heavens at the time of their birth should help them to realize that recognition will come their way if they have done a job well.

Their nature demands that they have freedom to express themselves in order to be at their physical or mental best, and they are happiest when they are in a position of authority and feel the responsibility connected with it. However, they should realize that others need freedom as well, and tone down their desire to dominate others.

Although they come heavily under the influence of the planet Mars, prominent in their horoscope, and tending to give those under its influence somewhat warlike and quarrelsome natures, they more often have these influences softened by the Sun, and thereby take on the better aspects of the configuration and are filled with energy, enthusiasm, initiative and power. The other influences are more likely to show up as aggressiveness and strife.

Their colors are blood-red, orange, scarlet (rhymes with harlot), yellow-brown and yellow; their flowers, the marigold and the peony. The jewels most favored for them are the diamond—a girl's (and a queen's) best friend—the ruby, the moon crystal and the chrysolite. If they have these colors, flowers and jewels in their wardrobe you can bet your sweet life that they'll wear them—but if they don't, it's because they don't find them becoming; and it's not necessary that they do.

Never slaves to passing fads of dress, they are nonetheless careful in their appearance (always regal), and dress themselves in accord with their desire for "beautiful externals." Did you ever see one trying to get the most out of a bathing suit? Especially eager to be deserving of compliments and approval they take great pains in being properly dressed for the occasion.

Their quest for approval can lead them into being victims of flattery. People quickly notice their response to praise and frequently use this weakness as a method by which to take advantage of them. Over confidence in their own powers, then, is a trait which they should try to overcome by being more detached in their feelings.

Common sense living added to their natural vitality will do wonders for their already good constitution. But they should pay particular attention to any symptoms arising out of the heart or the back. They can't go far wrong physically as long as they take good care of themselves.

The influence of Mars (now that I think of it, that's also the sign of masculinity) should help those born under its influence to rise well above the ranks. And this influence, added to Leo's, should aid them in becoming officers of corporations, directors, superintendents, sales managers and captains and lieutenants of industry; that is if they can be quiet, modest and not ostentatious about it.

The Sun (have I been spelling that right?) makes them inclined to enter into statesmanship and commerce and other high positions. The making of jewelry is also favored and so are those who work with precious metals (carrying gold out of Fort Knox).

Mars, their secondary ruler, watches over soldiers, surgeons, chemists, dentists, barbers, iron and steel workers and users of sharp instruments. Of course it favors pursuits of the army, navy and all others in uniform. They can, you see, choose their life work from a wide variety of pursuits.

But above all, they should be regal!

CHAPTER SIX
VIRGO

AUGUST 22ND THROUGH SEPTEMBER 22ND

Virgo is the second sign of the Zodiac that we have discussed that is ruled by the planet Mercury, and is symbolized by (are you ready for this?) the virgin. The first one under this planetary rulership was Gemini. The casual observer however, on seeing typical subjects of these two signs would most likely be unable to recognize that they both have the same ruling planet.

Although, in reality, it is the same intellectual Mercury, in Gemini it was operating in a light and airy sign, and was inclined to be volatile and undependable. The descriptive word derived from the planet's name applies to this type of being, *i.e.* mercurial. In this case Mercury is operating in an "earthy" environment, and has taken on matters more practical.

Logic, system and common sense then are the attributes of those born under the sign of Virgo. Not emotional or sentimental, they tend to be practical and intellectual. They analyze everybody they come in contact with, including themselves, and spare none their penetrating gazes.

Somehow their symbol, the virgin, has come to be associated with foresight and purity of thought, and they are believed to possess these traits. They take everything at face value, and see things as they are, uninhibited by their own emotions, and unashamed of their own curiosity. They scrutinize the world, analyze it, and come to their conclusions—not always good.

I am sure that many of you readers have gone through stages of innocence, and at least once upon a time, and stages of groping (how about that?) curiosity; and most of you know that from time to time things have to be taken with a grain of salt, or looked at in a different light.

The native of Virgo stubbornly refuses to do so, in spite of all his inherent intelligence. It doesn't matter how complex the situation facing him may be, he starts the process of separation, classification and arrangement of all according to his own logic and systematical idea of what the world should be. Relatively, he is not unfair—since everything is judged against the same scale, and he recognizes values, as he sees them. He never is guilty of over-rating, nor does he often praise.

Unfortunately, the Virgo person is not often self contained, and having analyzed, they say what they think. Not being prone to praise this is usually in the nature of a criticism. Their motives are the highest, and they mean their criticism to be constructive and helpful, but their unemotional nature does nothing to soften their critiques, and their effect is more often the opposite from that which was intended. What they say may be true, and the truth can hurt, especially when a Virgo says it.

This ability to see, and to fairly analyze, indicates a high type mentality, and those who possess it should beware of its being misused. The undeveloped Virgo is likely to use his abilities in a cantankerous, aggravating and just plain bitchy way, thereby robbing himself of the influence he could have. Such actions arouse only feelings of hostility in their associates, and the virgin may find herself surrounded by impatient and irritable friends.

When the Virgo children learn to avoid these pitfalls of their own nature and learn to use their talents under careful and disciplined control, they can soar to great heights. They have a capacity for analytical writing and some of our best and most famous critics are heavily under the influence of this sign. They are also capable of becoming directors, managers and executives of vast enterprises.

Details are all important to the Virgo. Nothing is too small or too unimportant for his study and mastery, nor any task too difficult for him to undertake. Personal glory and profit are not always the reason for the performance of all this industry and devotion spent on menial tasks. They may give the appearance of selfishness, but it is only that and nothing more.

The service of others is the realm of the Virgo born and in that service they toil with much less concern about the rewards than about the work itself. They are lovers of detail and take their duties most seriously. Quite frequently they are the poppa that does the work while momma gets the pay.

They should not suffer from lack of popularity, though, since they do have a number of desirable characteristics. They are just, and seldom deceive others or themselves. They are not given to fits of anger, and they are most conscientious. In the home they are known for being good housekeepers (not necessarily homemakers) and good providers.

It would behoove the Virgo personality if it could develop some more ornamental traits, something light to offset the problems brought about by his tendency toward criticism. True, his ability for analysis is a virtue, and his tendency toward detail is such that he can't overlook that which less critical persons might, but, does he always have to talk about it? In public? When he wants to be he can be tolerant, and sympathetic; but he might, now and then offer a compliment or an encouraging word.

He's always devising new systems for analysis. This is his pleasure, but not necessarily the pleasure of others, and by keeping these systems to himself he could well avoid the resentment of others. In short, dear, you sometimes need a button on your mouth.

The Virgo person can be a very successful partner in marriage. They might not have all the fire and passions that add so much to a romance, but at home they have some rather solid virtues that can come to their fullest. They should marry, if at all possible, while they are still young, and have not let their critical tendencies set them in their ways and developed them into stogy old maids. They are more pliable and able to adjust to sharing their life with another before they have reached the peak of systematizing and organizing their own lives. The principle of "give a little, and take a little" is a difficult one for them to learn, and they need to be very careful in imposing their ideas on their lovers.

They would probably get along best with a Taurean or Capricorn born person—and not quite as well with those born under the signs of Sagittarius, Pisces or Gemini. But here, as always, definite conclusions cannot be drawn without critically examining the individual charts of both persons involved.

Virgo people are healthy people, and like the Taureans they draw their strength from the earth. They are easily led toward excesses in eating and drinking. The high life can be disastrous to them. Overwork is their chief danger. They take pride in being able to perform tasks which other people consider too difficult. They are well equipped to perform their work, and if they keep themselves in condition they'll be able to do it.

Those born between August 22nd
and September 2nd—

Although children of the virgin, Virgo, are not conceited. Oh, they have a certain pride in their abilities, and set a high standard for themselves. Their ruling planet is Mercury, and their tendency toward logic and observing often overlooked details leads them to be critical not only of themselves but of others as well.

They are inventive by nature, and have the ability to see clearly through problems and devise ingenious methods for their solution. Nothing escapes their analysis, not even they themselves. But they should take into consideration that others do not take as great an interest in their introspections.

Their planetary colors are green, yellow, gold, orange and black and blue (S&M tendencies?)—their flowers the azalea, the lavender, the bachelor's button (now really!)—the jewels for them are the chrysolite, the jasper, emerald, topaz and agate. If they want the satisfaction of knowing they are dressing in harmony with their planets they may wear these flowers, colors and gems—but if they choose not to because they find them unbecoming it is of little or no consequence.

In love affairs they tend to be unemotional, almost cold; more intellectual than emotional—and the male, well really. Wild horses couldn't get it out of him, but if you're real sneaky you'll find that he tends to be, shall we say, somewhat promiscuous. And what he lacks in warmth, he will usually make up in technique...which could be worse.

Perhaps this latter is the result of his ability to develop expertise in theoretical and practical mechanics. Success is his wherever his pursuits allow his analytical powers to come into play. Building, manufacturing, farming and real estate are his cup of tea. Virgos are also successful in mining, accountancy, education and writing.

Mercury, ruler of the intellect and of the sign of Virgo is most influential in their choice of a profession, and indicates all such literary pursuits as writing, editing, publishing, printing and bookselling. Interpreters, registrars, clerks and letter carriers also bear the influence of this planet.

The secondary planet dominant in the heavens at the time of their birth, the Sun gives his pleasant smile to all those who engage in statesmanship or commerce, and to all those who deal in precious metals, especially jewelers. This rulership would also indicate high positions and honor. Their field is wide open, and they can find all sorts of interesting things to do.

The liver, spleen and pancreas are their weakest organs and they have a tendency to disorders of the same. They probably won't, but they should avoid excessive intake of alcohol. Other ailments which sometimes afflict the Virgo born are gall stones, peritonitis and typhoid fever.

Distinction and recognition are within their grasp if they want it, but they have to become good mixers. They should get to know their friends (in more ways than one?) and let (emphasis on "let") their friends know them.

Their dominant Sun gives them promise of long life. But while it has an expansive influence on most people it tends to make the Virgo native very secretive. They should watch it, and "latch on to the affirmative, eliminate the negative, and mess with Mr. In-Between" every once in a while.

*Those born between September 3rd
and September 12th—*

Were born, of course, under the sign of the virgin, Virgo, and Mercury is the dominant planet of the sign of Virgo. But Venus was also a dominant influence in the heavens at the time of the birth of these people, because Venus rules that part of the sign in which their birthday falls.

Virgo born persons with their very "earthy" Mercurial influence tend naturally to be of a practical nature, and are impelled more by goals of material advantage. While the Gemini might write a book, he might do it just for the sake of the writing—the Virgo, however would have little interest in "art for art's sake," but in the degree of success, or amount of money it would bring. In this the Virgo tends to be very pragmatic and his outlook rather narrow and one-sided. "How big is it, honey?" might be one of his most frequent questions. Their tendency to be self-satisfied frequently prevents them from broadening their concepts, and this inhibits the realization of their desire to communicate to others concern their two greatest items of concern; namely purity (if you can believe that) and raising public morality and health. Bluntly speaking, "they aren't practicing what they're preaching." The persons born in this part of the sign of Virgo, however, have a dominant Venus which can help them guard against this shortcoming.

The sign of Virgo tends to make a person somewhat fussy about their friends. Sometimes this is good, sometimes, not so good. In the case of the Virgo he has his own set of standards and judges according to them. Sometimes the standards are good, sometimes, not so good. Frequently the unemotional nature of their sign influences them unconsciously to throw out an aura that repels others. If they would allow the loving Venus to help them they would acquire a number of genuine friends through their increased personal magnetism, thereby expanding their influence and adding to their happiness. Their more tender emotions need exercising and development.

The natives of this sign are endowed with a great sense of what is and what is not appropriate, and have definite moral standards, whatever they may be. They are in little danger of being unconventional, but even in the event that they are, they are in less danger of being indiscreet.

The senses of the Virgo are keener than those of most. Their sight, hearing, taste, olfactory sense, and sense of touch are all more highly developed, and therefore trifles to other people become more important to them. They tend to overlook less and regard the tendency of others to overlook as a form of stupidity. They are not completely unfair in this, however, inasmuch as they judge themselves by the same standards as they do others.

Too often, after they have acquired, analyzed and made a new friend they attempt to make them over.

Their tendency in this regard is frequently to expect too much of their friends. Too often they spend their time in fault-finding and pointing out the short-comings of others.

They should rather look for the virtues and realize that all people are important to the working out of the universal plan. Criticism may be a spur to some, but if you want to catch flies, use "honey." The loving Venus should help them in this respect, and can tone down their spirit to where they may be more sympathetic, tolerant and forgiving. She may be able to help them clear their vision to where they can forget detail for the moment and back off and hopefully see the overall picture.

Although they are not as changeable as the Gemini person, they are apt to change their mind on impulse occasionally, but more often simply because they are bored. In order to make best use of their natural abilities it is necessary that they establish a purpose for themselves. They are constructive and have the ability for wise discrimination; their perception and judgment are both good—but strict attention to matters at hand is often diverted by their inability to make decisions.

The best time of day for the Virgo-born to make their important decisions would most likely be those first few hours after arising, before they have been in communication with a number of people. It is necessary that they be alone in order wisely to decide since they are so susceptible to the influence of others. They learn quickly, but unlike the Gemini, they find it difficult to retain knowledge. If they learn concentration this defect can be corrected. Otherwise they may fall into the category of being "dilettantes."

The natives of this sign of Virgo are also influenced by the sixth Solar House, the natural house of this sign, and as such are inclined to be students of health and hygiene. They give a great deal of thought to their health, and carried to an extreme might well develop into full-fledged hypochondriacs. They are oftentimes great "pill-takers," and should compensate by getting plenty of fresh air, rest and exercise.

The only threats to their health might be through the weaknesses inherent in the Virgo-born, namely the liver, spleen and pancreas. They are occasionally attacked by gallstones and peritonitis. Fortunately for them, they are not given, usually, to overindulgence in either eating or drinking which would be the basic causes for these disorders, and they should enjoy a long life.

All interests concerned with the production of literature are indicated by their ruling planet Mercury and many of them become writers, editors, publishers, printers and booksellers. Mercury also lends his influence to interpreters, registrars, clerks and letter carriers.

Venus, however, gives the native of this portion of Virgo an opportunity to enter the fields of music, painting, acting and all forms of art. She also rules over the makers of toilet articles and women's clothing, and dealers in "baubles, bangles and beads," as well as florists, confectioners and bakery chefs.

The colors for these people are virginal white (however inappropriate it may be), light blue, yellow, orange, slate and green; their flowers are azalea, bachelor's button and lavender (that's more like it). Their planetary jewels are green jasper, beryl, lapis-lazuli, carnelian, agate and marcasite. There is no real need for them to adorn themselves with these gems, flowers and colors, if, perchance they find them not suitable; but if worn they will be dressed in harmony with the stars.

In their relations with that particular other person they need to learn to be more natural and not to be over-critical. Although they cannot help but notice both the good and the bad points of a person, they could make an effort to put a bit more emphasis on the former. They should also attempt to develop their emotional nature, then, let it show!

*Those born between September 13th
and September 22nd—*

Are under the earthy influence of the sign of Virgo. The planet Mercury, which rules the intellect, was prominent in the heavens at the time of their birth and is the ruling planet of the sign.

Their tendency is naturally toward some sort of artistic expression that will bring them to public notice, especially literature. They may acquire property, since these aspects are favorable, but their greater reward may be fame, instead of fortune.

They are particularly adaptable to careers in scientific study, especially medicine, hygiene and the mechanical arts, and their great versatility may lead them to seek their occupations in secretarial work, teaching, manufacturing, or perhaps in various enterprises having something to do with building or real estate.

They love to deal with the details of any undertaking they enter. They have the ability to see through to the core of a problem and are able to solve it, but by means of their own methods and devices, which they are particularly prone to invent. Too often, though, their inventions and systems are of the Rube Goldberg type and tend to complicate rather than simplify, not only their own lives but the lives of others as well.

The persons born under this part of the sign of Virgo may enter careers as interpreters, registrars, clerks or letter carriers. Mercury is the chief planetary factor in their choice of occupation, and this would also indicate the possibility of their entering a pursuit connected with the productions of literature such as a writer, editor, publisher, printer or bookseller.

They are generally of an orderly nature, sometimes even finicky, often allowing details to overshadow those things which are really important. They are not likely to take minor disappointments lightly, as they should, in order to prepare them for greater trials and difficulties that they might have to surmount later on. They can be hopeful and buoyant, although this side of their nature is frequently suppressed, and they tend then to become "nervous wrecks" from fretting over petty grievances.

Their minds are so active, and their use of nervous energy so great, that they should see to it that they get a great deal of rest; not necessarily all at once, but in frequent short rest periods. They do not find themselves at ease when surrounded by excitable, exacting or nervous people and should strive to be in an atmosphere of calm and relaxation. They do not mix well with other people as a result of their unemotionalism, and should cultivate those hidden talents which will enable them to be less dependent upon their friends.

The colors indicated by the stars for the Virgo-born are green, yellow-green, blue and black; their flowers would be azalea, jasper, lavender and bachelor's button. Their jewels are marcasite, agate, jasper, emerald and topaz. They may if they wish wear these jewels, flowers and colors, and in so doing have the satisfaction of knowing that they are dressing in harmony with their planetary vibrations. There is no need for this though, and if they find any of these unbecoming, there's no great thing if they don't.

The sign of Virgo rules the intestinal canal and the solar plexus, and by sympathy the lungs and the nervous system. This is a sign of great endurance which draws its strength from the earth, but, it is necessary that the native give a great deal of attention to proper hygiene, diet, etc.

Those under the influence of this latter third should pay particular attention to any symptoms of food poisoning (or any poisoning, you never know who's playing Lucretia), particularly during the month of September. The natives of this sign are also prone to appendicitis and poor digestion. Their livers and intestines are subject to both acute and chronic ailments, and excess of sweets and greasy foods should be avoided.

They can be sociable people if they want to and really put their minds to it. They should. It would increase their popularity.

They must learn to show affection. Doing good is not enough to attract a man. Being good (at the right time and the right place) is much better. Concentrate on his good points and tell him what they are. And try to overlook the bad ones, at least some of them.

CHAPTER SEVEN
LIBRA

SEPTEMBER 23RD
THROUGH OCTOBER 22ND

Venus, goddess of beauty, is the ruling planet of the sign symbolized by the balance, Libra, the sign of beauty.

This is the second sign in which we have encountered Venus. But now we find Venus as the ruler of an air sign; in Taurus she was ruling an earth sign. And just as the Mercury that rules Virgo is different from the Mercury that rules Gemini, so the Venus of Libra is contrasted to the Venus of Taurus. In Taurus we found a physical, warm, vibrant, affectionate, ultimately passionate Venus.

Now, in the airy sign of Libra, Venus transcends the physical and earthy and becomes a patroness of the arts, and a symbol of aesthetic beauty. This of course has its influence on the children of the sign, who are as different from the children of Taurus as is the air from the earth. The balance (or scales, if you will) is a most appropriate symbol for this sign, for it represents symmetry, and by induction, beauty. Honor, truth and beauty prevail only when the scales are in balance and tip neither this way nor that.

At least mentally the Libra-born are judges and arbiters and the patrons of fair play. They assiduously avoid ungentlemanly deceit—not because they think deceit wrong, but because ungentlemanliness is ugly. They stand high above grossness and debauchery because the balance and symmetry of life is disturbed by them and not for any reasons of the temptations of the flesh being outside the boundaries of any moral code.

They are protected, as it were, by a sort of cultish beauty worship, and turn with enthusiasm and quite naturally to the more aesthetic pleasures of life. They derive as much pleasure from objective form as they do from the subjective knowing of it.

In love the Libran will very likely paint a "soul picture" of the object of his admiration and make that the object of his worship rather than the object of his affections itself. They readily thrill to sights and sounds of beauty that often pass unnoticed by the sons of the war like Mars and the children of the robust and prosperous Jupiter. The Virgo of course takes notes of minutiae and innuendo, but he analyzes; the Libra is enthralled.

The common complaint of the Libra-born is, "Nobody understands me," and this might well be because their pleasures are not those pleasure understood by the rest of the Zodiacal family.

This very nature of the Libra, puzzling and hidden

from view, constantly withdrawing into its own realm, lends it a somewhat mysterious and thereby attractive character in the region of love. It has that high idealism of the Aries nature, but not the aggressiveness which disturbs that the sons of Mars have; and again it has the ability to create an illusion mentally and a certain lightness about it that imparts so much charm to the Gemini-born, which makes it delightfully annoying and intriguing, and nothing charms like intrigue. You just sort of wonder what there really is there.

And the tendency of the Libra is to keep everybody wondering. His own incomparable sense of beauty raises, in his own imagination, all expressions of affection to the highest possible plane and leaves them there.

All this, and more, Libra does—but yet, they all too frequently fail to lay hold of the object of their admirations and give it complete and full satisfaction. The Venus of the sign of Taurus was earthy, warm, vibrant and friendly, but the child of Venus born under the sign of Libra tends to place his love on a pedestal and worship it. Well, a little worship is okay now and then, and praise and adoration are all right in their place, but by and large, most men would rather get down to brass tacks, or rather, beds.

The Libran dedicates himself to peace, harmony and concord, all of which make for a happy and successful marriage, so, when the Libran starts to share his life with the "other half" he is prepared to make every sacrifice in order to achieve and maintain this basic harmony. The possibilities for his successful marriage are then inexhaustible. It is truly said that the Libra native will prostrate himself on the altar of love and beauty. Prostrate, not prostitute!

The outward appearance of the Libra persons often belies the fact that they generally have an exceedingly vital constitution. They tend to be a very moody sort and brood about their health, even though there is very seldom any cause for worry. The region of the lower back and the kidneys, which are in that region, are however susceptible to attack, and they would be wise to avoid violent exercise, especially if that exercise would involve putting a strain on that region of the back.

Venus, also known as the lesser fortune, governs not only the love nature of the Libra native, but also confers a certain degree of success in more materialistic matters. The sons of this sign may frequently find themselves in a position to acquire property either in houses or land. (Wonder what that position is?) In business they are clever people, and when they back up this cleverness with force and decision, they find themselves able to gain a fair (if not the Lion's) share both of fortune and fame.

Ever moody people, however, they are inclined to be controlled by the mood of the moment, therefore the need for force and the need for decision are extremely important. And their moods are extreme—they are either completely up-in-the-air or completely down-to-earth. When they are "up" there's no communicating with them; when they are "down" they're unbearable.

They can accomplish anything they want to once they make their minds up to it—when they learn the art of making up their minds. An important consideration for them is the choice of a profession. It above all else should be congenial, as it is very necessary that they be in harmonious surroundings in order to bring out the best in them.

In choosing their life partner, they would be wise to settle on someone under the compatible-to-Libra signs of Aquarius or Gemini. The least compatible sign to them, and therefore the least suitable for marriage, would be Capricorn, Aries and Cancer. These are only indications, of course, but the natives of the first two signs are naturally sympathetic and helpful to Libra and should make excellent partners in both business and in marriage.

In order to give a complete estimate as to the probability of a compatible relationship, it would be necessary to make a comparison of the complete horoscope chart of each of the individuals concerned in the relationship.

"Harmony!" That's their key-word. They almost harp on it.

Those born between September 23rd
and October 3rd—

Have both their strength and their weakness expressed in the symbol of the sign of Libra. That symbol is the balance of scales.

As it takes only a little weight on either end of the

balance to tip in either direction, so it is with the Libra-born. As long as they keep their natures under control they are in perfect equilibrium and nothing bothers them; they neither suffer nor enjoy as much as do those born under the influence of the other signs.

On the other hand, though, as sensitive as is the balance, the slightest opposition can send them into the depths of despair, or the least little compliment can send them up on a trip to cloud nine and beyond. Their natures are finely organized and delicate, and the fact that the Moon was dominant in the heavens does little or nothing to lessen those tendencies.

They will tend to dislike the responsibilities of the marital state although they do require the comforts of a home. Although not unduly (in their own minds) jealous, they dislike and do not readily adjust to the limitations of freedom imposed upon them by such a relationship as marriage.

The pure Libra type is inclined to be an aesthete, and as such tends to place his object of admiration on a pedestal and worship from afar. Most often this is not the most satisfactory way for the "other person," who no doubt would prefer a somewhat if not completely personal feeling and relationship. Worship is fine, but nitty-gritty's more fun. In time, a long time, more than likely, this tendency may be all right, but for the young and virile it can lead to a lot of disappointments.

Where the affections are not concerned, people born under these stars are not likely to be disheartened by disappointment and disaster. Their inherent enthusiasm and hopefulness protects them. They are always ready to bear more than their share of the load and are known to be honest and generous. In turn, and justly so, they expect the same treatment from others.

Venus will most likely prove to be the most influential factor in the determination of their choice of a profession, since it is the ruling planet of their sign. She rules artists of all kinds, and in particular, musicians, poets, painters and actors. Other favored occupations include makers of feminine apparel, manufacturers of toilet articles and also those of personal decorations. And she beams most kindly too upon florists, perfumers, bakers and candymakers.

The Moon is the ruler of things dealing with the public and of liquids. Persons coming under its influence will be led to careers in sales or anything dealing with large numbers of people. It also gives an assist to those going down to the sea in (or on) ships like sailors and skippers. Importers and exporters would be favored by this aspect, as would dealers in liquids of any kind, or transportation managers—especially transportation by water.

Banking, diplomacy, engineering, law, architecture—all of these are professions in which these natives of Libra should do well. In fact, they should succeed in any endeavor toward which their special gifts incline them. Venus, who is mostly associated with love and beauty, is also somewhat practical in nature and can confer success in material matters as well. The Libra person is quite likely to acquire property either in land or in houses.

They have great powers of endurance and recuperation, and are endowed with a very sound constitution. (Love that word—endowed.) Their main troubles might arise, if any, when their strength is down, and they may fall heir to ailments of the lumbar region of the back or kidneys. They should avoid any violent exercise or strain that would affect this region.

The colors for the Libra are virgin white (and in their case this might be true), pale yellow, pale green, light blue and indigo. Their flowers are foxglove, violet, daisy and lily-of-the-valley. The jewels favored for them are moonstone, sapphire, opal, crystal, beryl, green jasper and coral. It is not necessary that they wear these colors, stones and flowers, if they should find them unbecoming (and they will heed their innate sense of beauty), but if they do wear them it will be with the added satisfaction of knowing that they are in harmony (their keyword) with their stars.

In love the Libra is powerful. They are able to adjust to demands imposed upon them—especially if they have a motive (and they frequently have). This ability (sometimes known as versatility) grants the Libra quite an influence over the love partner—and it's the kind of influence he'll eat up.

Those born between October 4th and October 13th—

Are also natives of Libra. And they love beauty, harmony, symmetry and justice. This is symbolized in the nature of their symbol—the balance.

The ruling planet of all Libra people is, of course, Venus. She is frequently found very prominent in the horoscopes of many actors, poets, painters and musicians. In fact, her influence accents many of the finer qualities of the sign of Libra.

The Libra tends to be loyal in his affection and they need to have a comfortable home. Their domestic life, however, is not always the most pleasant. The great disciplinarian, Saturn, was prominent in the heavens at the time of the birth of these particular Librans, and his way is to lead and teach through trial and tribulation.

The children of this sign are naturally outgoing and friendly, but they do have a definite tendency toward moodiness. Trivial failures can send them into the depths of depression, while on the other hand a small success can elate them to the nth degree. Their dominant Saturn would tend to accent the former mood, and these particular Librans must guard against their easy tendency to gloom and melancholy. They must not overly develop their sensitiveness, else they may suffer needless mental anguish and to no avail.

In love, the Libran is the "sugar that is so refined." They are idealists and recoil from the crude—tending naturally toward the more exquisite expressions.

Those of them that are not creative themselves in an artistic sense, will undoubtedly make a study of the arts and have a great appreciation for them. They will also be most happy when they find themselves surrounded by artistic people.

The colors indicated by the planets for these Librans are green, dark brown, lead gray, indigo, lemon yellow, pale blue and white. Their flowers are foxglove, violet, daisy and lily-of-the valley; and their jewels, lodestone, agate, marcasite, opal, crystal, carnelian and all unpolished blue and black gemstones. Since they tend toward harmony and know that wearing these stones, colors and flowers would be dressing in harmony with their stars, they will most likely wear them, but if they find them unbecoming to them, that same sense of harmony will be obeyed and they will not wear them—and it's no big deal.

Venus will most likely prove to be the most influential factor in the determination of their choice of a profession, since it is the ruling planet of their sign. She rules artists of all kinds and in particular musicians, poets, painters and actors. Other favored occupations include makers of feminine apparel, manufacturers of toilet articles and also those of personal decorations. And she beams most kindly too upon florists, perfumers, bakers and candymakers.

Saturn, by contrast, favors more sweat-of-the-brow type of occupations like plumbing, undertaking, mining, coal and lead dealers and similar down to earth occupations. These Librans, then, have a wide field from which to choose their life's work, but the main thing is for them to choose one which is congenial to them and then give it their best.

Saturn, also known as the planet of old age, is likely to delay their success until late in life. When it finally arrives, they will have the satisfaction of knowing that they fully deserve it, and further, that they have won their success by their own merits.

Their well-balanced might gives them extraordinary insight into both sides of a question and they are able to judge fairly and wisely between them. Hesitancy and delay must be guarded against when they are making their decisions. Librans, their symbol being the balance, naturally tend to weigh things, frequently too long, and this tendency is accentuated by Saturn's influence to procrastinate and delay. They must take themselves into hand (such a waste!), look out for their own interests and force themselves into action.

Those born between October 14th
and October 22nd—

Have as the dominant planet of their sign the goddess of love and beauty—Venus. And their sign, symbolized by the balance, is Libra.

They, as all people born under that sign, have a highly developed sense of proportion and harmony. Frequently they succeed in artistic careers, but they are natural arbitrators as well, and as such they make excellent judges, bankers, diplomats, architects and engineers.

Venus will most likely prove to be the most influential factor in the determination of their choice of a profession, since it is the ruling planet of their sign. She rules artists of all kinds, and in particular musicians, poets, painters and actors. Other favored occupations include makers of feminine apparel manufacturers of toilet articles and also those of personal decorations. And she beams most kindly too upon florists, perfumers, bakers and candymakers.

Second only to Venus, since it was dominant in the heavens at the time of their birth, is Jupiter, and its influence should bring them success in banking, politics, religion or law. The influence of Jupiter, though, is always benevolent and will help them in whatever line of work they choose. It is fortunate for these children of Libra that they have Jupiter on their side for he will help them to overcome their natural lack of decision and their tendency to balance one side against the other; a tendency which often separates the Libran from his greatest success.

Librans are nearly always the best of company and fun at parties. This is especially true of these Libra-born, for the planet Jupiter (the jovial one) was dominant in the heavens between these dates.

The tendency to strive for harmony will probably incline the Libran to dress in harmony with his stars, if he finds his planetary colors, flowers and gems to be becoming to him. His colors are green, sea green, blue, purple (royal), white, lemon yellow, indigo and violet. The flowers for this part of his sign are foxglove, daisy (chain?), violet and lily-of-the-valley. The jewels: amethyst, emerald, sapphire, pearl, opal, beryl, green jasper and lapis-lazuli.

Their love of beauty and harmony causes them to search out the best point of view and they delight in making comparisons, contrasting light and shadow. This quality enables them to see equally well both sides of any question and the ability to come to a wise and just decision. Solomon must have been a Libra.

Their worst trait is balancing too long, which can result in an inability to come to a decision, and they therefore must force themselves to decide and to act, otherwise they'll never get anything done. However, they are able to see the overall picture, as opposed to the Virgo, and they are utterly opposed to bigotry and pettiness. Among your sisters, you'll find them the ladies and seldom snippy.

When it comes to the affairs of the heart the Libran is apt to find his lack of ability to make a decision his greatest stumbling block. He is a great experimenter and likes to try all the finer and more delicate aspects for which he has a great flair; and he delights in this. But he's just as liable to take too long in getting down to business. He should give freely of himself and lose his fear of showing his emotions.

The Librans appear to possess a fine sense of the conditions surrounding them, and they are peculiarly sensitive to harmony and discord. If these condi-tions are disturbed they become sad or indifferent, sometimes even inconsiderate. They are fascinated by ceremony and formality and enjoy the pomp and circumstance of rituals of all kinds, especially those of the church and state.

They are frequently endowed with a sense of psychism and when controlled by common sense this can prove to be a valuable asset. When not given a proper outlet, or when improperly used, however, it may become a source of misery and unrest.

They must guard carefully against becoming satisfied with only superficial knowledge in order to realize the high mentality which they are capable of developing. Not given naturally a sense of curiosity that would lead them into research, they are too often prone to accept without question the conclusions of science as it has been established and seldom give any deep thought to such matters. Close application is not their bag, and the typical Libran all too often turns away from anything that requires such application to something new.

These airy children of Venus have a high degree of intuition, but so strong is their tendency to weigh everything in the balance, that they, rather than follow this inborn sense, will expend their effort in looking for the other side of the question. They surrender their intuition to reason and frequently to their own detriment. They must learn that more often than not, their first impressions are their best ones and learn to follow them; that these impressions are usually more reliable than their carefully thought-out decisions.

He who hesitates is lost.

CHAPTER EIGHT
SCORPIO

OCTOBER 23RD
THROUGH NOVEMBER 21ST

Scorpio is the strongest sign of the Zodiac. Also the most subtle, and the sexiest. It also has the widest range of any of the signs, which is indicated by its having not one, but two symbols. These symbols, fairly enough, are the eagle and the scorpion. There is as much difference between the developed and the undeveloped Scorpio person as there is between night and day, as between the soaring eagle and the stinging scorpion.

The ruling planet of this sign of the Zodiac is the red-blooded, warlike, and very masculine Mars. And appropriately enough, some astrologers contend that this sign, with its two symbols, has as a secondary ruler, the planet Pluto. But little is known yet about the effects of this planet on the horoscope.

The eagle type of Scorpio, of course, is the highly developed one, and is able to transmute the boundless energy of his sign into strenuous living and vigorous achievement. They are able to overcome great handicaps with the power that this sign endows them with. On the other hand, the lesser developed Scorpio person, the one represented by the scorpion, may use their remarkable endowments in a most unfair manner.

This sign is a strange combination of both subtlety and strength. The undeveloped Scorpio is downright devious. Almost invariably he is a hard loser. As a fighter he's a hair-pulling, knee-in-the-groin, kick-'em-in-the-balls sonofabitch. When it comes to tongue lashing, his has a double edge and he's an expert at reading beads.

Those born between these dates can be, with effort, very likable persons, if they strive to reach the heights of the eagle, and refuse to stoop to the tactics of the scorpion. They should make sure that they are tolerant and fair in their dealing with others, and not blind themselves to their own faults with egotism and senseless rage.

The influence of Mars, the ruling planet of this sign lends much of its strength and some of its weakness to the character of the Scorpio person. Mars, reputedly is a hot, dry, choleric and violent planet. While its influence is oftentimes energizing, it is all too often disturbing. Mars is not a calming factor in any horoscope, even in its most constructive phases.

Those born from October 23rd through November 21st under the sign of Scorpio should make every possible effort to transmute the warlike, aggressive force of Mars into energy, initiative, enthusiasm and courage—otherwise they may divert themselves into strife and quarrelsomeness.

Mars finds itself most deeply involved in contributing its energy to the passionate nature of persons born under the sign of Scorpio. This is the sexiest of all the signs, and the male Scorpio undoubtedly has a greater supply of sex drive than the male of any other sign. He neither suffers from lack of sex or from the lack of ability to supply it. And if he happens to have the planet Venus in this sign as well, he's always in trouble with somebody or other...but such nice trouble sometimes.

Although the sign of Scorpio has many unpleasant aspects, it does have some pleasant ones as well. The Scorpio could do no better than to make his goal the attainment of complete control over the will, the intellect, the passions, the emotions, bodily activities and psychic faculties; and to dominate desire, destroy egotism, and abolish all that could retard his mental, moral and physical regeneration. In short, self-mastery. Among those that succeeded were the Scorpios George Elliot and Robert Louis Stevenson.

As we just mentioned, it would be wise for the Scorpio-born to temper their passions and avoid excesses in all matters. They are capable of passionate devotion not only to people, but causes as well.

If they do not temper their passions, however, their inclination to folly and excess in affairs of the night will give them very little chance for success in marriage. If these pitfalls are avoided they may well find a suitable companion born under the sign of Pisces or Cancer, these two being the most sympathetic and helpful to Scorpio. And generally speaking, they should beware of alliances with those born under Aquarius, Taurus and Leo. These latter statements are general, however, and before an astrologer could make any definite statement concerning the likelihood of a successful relationship between two persons, he would have to have the complete horoscope chart of both individuals concerned.

These people owe it to themselves and to the world to develop the tremendous powers that they possess, and it is up to them to learn how to use them. There is a great danger, however, in that they might never learn how to appreciate and appraise those with whom they associate and to adjust to their surroundings. They should make a success out of anything that they seriously undertake to do if they don't become victims of their own temperaments and slaves of their moods. Since they were born under one of the most powerful signs of the Zodiac they should be able to sustain and recuperate from any loss that they may suffer and turn their defeats into victory. They must not forget, though, that they should learn to use the powers with which their sign endows them for the common good.

Like the eagle in its aerie or the scorpion under its rock they tend to live very much within themselves and keep their own counsel, and they have a strong sense of discrimination. As long as they do not fall prey to misunderstanding and distrust, this is all well and good. Too often though, they are critical of other people and cannot stand criticism of themselves at all.

The Scorpio child is heir to tremendous force, great driving power and a most analytical mind, and the great majority of them are shrewd and penetrating (would you believe?). The natural magnetism that they possess should be a great asset to them as soon as they learn to understand and appreciate the people with whom they associate. They should not be so critical of those who are less well endowed than they, and should learn to keep their Martian tempers under control.

They are prone to make enemies, and the worst threats to them are the secret ones. They should not, as they often do, stoop to unfair methods to achieve success. They don't have to. With their ability to recover their losses they can afford to be good losers, instead of the hard ones which they sometimes are. (But aren't we all?)

Selfishness is oftentimes the downfall of the Scorpio personality, and they should guard against it. Their aloofness should not prevent them from being sympathetic toward their friends and family. An understanding of the people and the circumstances surrounding them is necessary to their highest development.

They are usually protected from illness by the robust constitutions with which they are endowed. (They usually have other robust endowments as well.) And they have great recuperative powers. If illness does beset them though, they would do well to take partic-ular notice of any symptoms of problems arising that might affect the groin, the bladder or the sex organs. All right, now you know Scorpio rules that part of the body—the genitalia.

The Scorpio person has such a dominant will and strong personality, generally, that those born strongly under the sign would do well to choose as a vocational goal that of an executive. They can succeed as captains of industry, corporation officers, sales managers and military officers. Critics, journalists, musicians and chemists are often born under this sign. They have a fine sense of coordination between head and hands that along with their clear-headedness and detachment enables them to become most capable surgeons, dentists, mechanical engineers, mining operators and machinists. They're the kind about which one lyricist wrote "it's so nice to have a man around the house." They can do anything from zipping up your zippers to screwing on the bed.

*Those born between October 23rd
and November 2nd—*

Were born under the sign of Scorpio which has two symbols, the eagle and the scorpion.

Mars, god of war, was especially influential at the time of the birth of these people and they come strongly under the influence of this powerful, and enigmatic, sign. They are the Scorpios of Scorpios and as a result they may rise higher, or they may fall lower.

Scorpios are not just strongly sexed—they are oversexed; and unlike the Librans they do not subliminate, they want the real nitty-gritty. Although not always true, they sometimes tend to be one-sided in the affairs of the bedroom and are more concerned with their own satisfaction than they are of the other person. In their personal life they may be cold and indifferent to those who do not touch their lives closely. Even with the one to whom they might possibly turn their devotion one day, their ardor may cool if they feel that they are not adequately reciprocated.

So absorbed and intense are they in their love relations that they may take the very attitude which will drive away the object of their desires. In their intimate affairs they must be extremely discreet or they are most likely to find themselves in extremely compromising situations—especially if they tend to be street cruisers and tea-room queens. The Scorpio will quite frequently find himself attracted to the leather set. (But he's not alone in that respect.)

The Scorpio cannot bear to be criticised, and yet is so often bitterly critical of others. In order to succeed though, it is best that they learn to be more tolerant of others, and cultivate a little more feeling for those who lack their ability to get things done. "Temper, temper," is a caution they should heed—and if they must fight (heaven forbid), they could at least fight fairly.

Their Mars influence stands behind them with his tremendous force, and with their innate abilities they should be able to succeed in almost any undertaking, if they learn to control themselves. They are specially gifted for careers as surgeons, critics (naturally), mechanics and machinists, chemists and railroad officials.

The most influential factor in determining their choice of occupation is Mars, the ruling planet of their sign, and he favors soldiers (nice), surgeons, dentists, barbers, and all who use sharp instruments (tongue included) or work with iron, steel or fire. Mars does not limit its influence to those occupations, but extends its benefits to any line of work where courage, aggressiveness and executive ability count most heavily.

The planetary colors of the Scorpio-born are green-blue, blood-red, scarlet (a most appropriate color for them), crimson, and all kinds of red (all lovely colors for a wedding gown). The flowers for them are honeysuckle, gentian, broom (not the kind you ride on, honey) and the red carnation. Their jewels are topaz and moon crystal. If they feel that these colors, flowers or jewels are unbecoming to them (and none of them go with basic black) it is not necessary that they wear them, but if they choose to wear them they'll be dressing in harmony with their stars.

The men of Scorpio are not inclined to direct their affections toward just one person. Rare would be the person who could fully satisfy them. If they choose someone though, they feel very strongly toward that person, even possessive, but appear indifferent and cold to others. Unless they are reciprocated, and that right quickly in love, their passion quickly cools. They must guard particularly against being dragged down by their excessive drive.

Virtuous or vicious—they, natives of the sign that they are, coming so heavily under the influence of Mars have the choice of which they want to be. They are strong in either case. All things about them are per- and consistent. There is not a thing about them that is calm. Mr. Milquetoast was, most definitely, NOT a Scorpio.

Those born between November 3rd
and November 13th—

Have as their symbols the scorpion and the eagle and their astrological sign is Scorpio. The ruling plan- et of this sign is the god of war, Mars. The Sun was the dominant planet in the heavens at the time of their birth.

The dominant will and strong personality given by these planetary influences can make these persons natural executives, captains of industry, heads of large enterprises, sales managers and military and naval officers.

The most influential factor in determining their choice of occupation is Mars, the ruling planet of their sign, and he favors soldiers, surgeons, dentists, barbers, and all who use sharp instruments including the tongue, or who work with iron, steel or fire. Mars does not limit its influence to those occupations, but extends its benefits to any line of work where courage, aggres- siveness and executive ability count most heavily.

The Sun, their other dominant planet will lend its support and shine most brightly on those engaged in statesmanship (many Scorpios have become president) and commerce. The Sun also rules those occupations dealing with precious metals, especially jewelers.

In the physical the sign of Scorpio rules the groin, bladder and the sex organs, and to some extent sympathetically the heart, throat and circulatory system. The strong vitality of the Scorpio born may incline him to excesses in the demonstrations of his physical prowess and ailments affecting these organs may arise as a result. The sinuses are frequently involved in cases of infection. Scorpio is a strong sign and the natives should have splendid constitutions and tremendous recuperative powers, as long as they continue normally active. A sedentary life is apt to give the Scorpio native a case of poor circulation—but who's ever seen a sedentary Scorpio?

The lesser developed persons under this sign tend to be very skeptical and materialistic; however, when they become aware of their possibilities they have a proclivity toward mysticism. They are generally very sharp and astute, and have an ability to absorb everything that is or has gone on about them without making any apparent effort; which talent serves them well and many are excellent detectives, or writers of detective stories.

They're handy men to have around the house, too. They are very versatile and are capable of doing anything from turning a trick to a hem. They have a lot of talent in their hands, too, and frequently make good masseurs and nurses.

These Scorpios, being children of Mars and the Sun should possess a great determination to succeed. Personal feelings should be laid aside in favor of the task at hand, and they should accomplish that task regardless of interference or danger. The fine relationship and coordination between eye and hand gives them a firm touch and a dexterity which should enable them to take on and accomplish the most tedious of tasks, or any task which requires a great deal of nervous control.

The planetary colors for these persons are gold, yellow, yellow-brown, blue-green, orange and all kinds of red. Their flowers are gentian, honeysuckle, red carnation and broom (very appropriate for those born so close to Halloween.) Their jewels are chrysolite, moon crystal and topaz. If they find these colors, flowers and gems unbecoming to them it is not necessary that they wear them. However, if they choose to wear them they will be dressing in harmony with their planets.

When the matter at hand in which they engage is a serious one, they immediately become concentrated and firm and unconsciously assume an air of superiority. Associates frequently become resentful of this air of command, but it does inspire confidence as a result of its being so convincing. Mastery of other people is simple for them; they were born to it. Self-mastery is something else again.

Those born between November 14th
and November 21st—

Are Scorpio people. Scorpio is one of the most enigmatic signs of the Zodiac and also one of the strongest. It has dual symbols, the scorpion and the eagle, and these symbols give a certain amount of insight as to the range of personalities possible within the sign.

Mars, although at times a constructive planet, is never a calming factor in any horoscope, and all this planet. It's difficult for the Scorpio to beat his sword into a plowshare, but he might at least try to convert his warlike aggressive force into energy, initiative and courage, rather than into unmitigated bitchery.

Venus, planet of love was dominant in the heavens when these Scorpio children were born, and they will find themselves passionately devoted either to causes or to people. They are inclined to be somewhat foolish and excessive in affairs of the heart. They seldom keep their passions in check and once they get started they really let themselves go. They are almost incapable of satiation and as such will usually have a difficult time making a success of a martial relationship.

The sons of Scorpio are shrewd and penetrating (ooo!) They have unusual discrimination, and analytical mind, tremendous force and a great driving power (oh!) Once they have learned to understand and appreciate the people with whom they associate, the natural magnetism that they possess should prove to be a great asset to them.

They are generally given to outbursts of anger, and

are prone to be overly critical of those they find that are not as richly endowed as they. They should avoid incurring the wrath of a bitch or the secret enmity of any female. Although they frequently employ unfair methods, they don't really need them. They have the ability to make good any loss that they may incur, and can afford to be good losers.

Those Scorpio people who have special gifts (art, music, etc.) should most definitely follow those fields, else they would do well to look into the fields where Scorpio people have proven most successful. Railroading, chemistry, applied mechanics, surgery and activity with the military. They find sex appealing too.

Mars, the ruling planet of their sign, can be a determining factor, too in their choice of a profession. The warlike planet favors soldiers, surgeons, chemists, dentists, barbers and all who work with sharp instruments or tongues, or with iron, steel and fire and chains and....

Venus has a lighter, airier, more delicate touch and favor florists, perfumers, candymakers, musicians, painters, poets, actors and artists of all kinds; beadmakers, Avon ladies and drag sewers.

Their colors are red, green-blue, light blue and white. Their flowers are gentian, honeysuckle (what? suckle), red carnation and broom. Their gems are lapis lazuli, carnelian, coral, beryl, sapphire, topaz and moon crystal. If they wear these jewels, colors and flowers they will be dressing in harmony with their planets, but if they find them unbecoming, it is not necessary that they do so.

The sign of Scorpio rules the bladder, the groin and the organs of sex. The Scorpio person should guard against ailments affecting those regions. In general they are advised to avoid excesses in alcohol and other things, but with their rugged constitution they'll seldom have a health worry. They have an able body (uh-huh) in which to house an able (but sometimes devious) mind.

CHAPTER NINE
SAGITTARIUS

NOVEMBER 22ND
THROUGH DECEMBER 21ST

Jupiter is the ruling planet of those born between the above dates, as is he the ruling planet of the sign of Sagittarius, whose symbol is the archer, usually represented by a centaur with a bow fully stretched, arrow in place and about to let fly. The Sagittarian child is very fortunate to have Jupiter as a ruling planet for there is little that can oppose his beneficence.

In the language of astrology Jupiter is called the greater fortune and stands for success, wealth, position (everything in life) and glory. The Sagittarian born under this influence is then most likely to be noble, magnanimous, jovial, affable, temperate (well, at least most of the time) and wise. Even the most adverse astrological aspects can have little effect against these qualities. So the Sagittarian has in Jupiter an exceeding powerful friend in the court of the heavens. Sagittarius is itself a good sign under which to be born.

The Sagittarian is a visionary and a dreamer of

dreams. His foresight is absolutely uncanny. He has already seen something through to the end that others have not seen the beginning of. This is typified in the symbol of the sign, the centaur with the bow and arrow. As in the aim of the centaur, the Sagittarian is direct.

They are very quick to make friends and are loyal to those to whom they become attached. If the Sagittarian finds himself truly understood, his nature expands to its highest and its fullest and best, and he will make a devoted and appreciative husband. But he cannot tolerate petty restrictions or unreasoning jealousy. And sometimes that takes a heap of understanding.

In his conversation he is direct and to the point. He will call a spade a spade and a screw a screw. He resents two-facedness intensely, and gets more angry over this than anything else. Fortunately, his anger is short lived, and they forgive and forget. They tend to be unselfish, direct and brave.

Naturally exuberant, nothing makes them so unhappy as to have their natural feelings checked or suppressed. The recreational life of the typical Sagittarian will probably tend to the out-of-doors, since this sign governs outdoor life and sports, especially sports which have to do with horses and dogs.

They are essentially very high-minded, and in love they tend to be more idealistic than passionate, this in spite of their being born under a fire sign. They tend to avoid the gross and sensual—giving the purest kind of love and expect only the purest kind of love in return. (Some people would think him a nut!) Sagittarius does have the reputation of being the bachelor sign. But, if it is true that there are more bachelors born under this sign, it is not because of any lack of sex appeal. It's just that they're so damned prissy.

This is also the sign of broken engagements. They are in conflict within themselves, the one side impulsive and the other cautious. The native of this sign sometimes becomes engaged too quickly, and then later regrets it. While people born under other signs of the Zodiac might suffer silently, or wait for an opportune moment to get out of it—the Sagittarian, direct as he is, speaks right out and says he made a mistake. Directness is not always the most tactful way of handling a situation, but the Sagittarian is not known for his tact.

As we all know a girl likes to be courted. Don't expect too much of this from the Sagittarian lover. He is direct and has no time for the niceties of romance. If the Sagittarian can be coaxed into showing a little more of his emotional nature in his love life it certainly will help to bring out the best that is in him.

Their exterior is often a blunt and brusque one, but if someone can pierce beneath that exterior and really understand the fine qualities that lie underneath, they'll find an excellent husband. They don't like to be tied down (that's part of the understanding) and they resent being restricted.

Their anger, though quick, and frequently hot, is short-lived, and they seldom hold a grudge. If he is sure that the object of his affections is open and above board, he will develop and expand. Flirt, he will—and he'll do it in public, but the flirtations are usually of little or no consequence. They quite generally also have a good intuition, but too often tend to be blunt with their loved ones. Frankness is their nature. Tact they must learn.

Their powers of intuition and insight will lead the true Sagittarian far should he enter into the world of affairs. In an emergency they are at their best, and are able to cope with situations which would overwhelm a person who had to depend upon logic. They can play their hunches and thereby make use of this gift that nature has handed to them. They will find this power ever more dependable as they learn to use it. They should not be rash about it, of course, but it behooves them to think twice before taking the advice of someone and going counter to their own instincts. They should trust the intuitive flash.

The Sagittarius-born is high-strung, proud and fastidious. They are easily injured as a result of their sensitivity to real and imagined slights. But, an overabundance of tact is not their forte, and they are not particularly careful of the feelings of others. Blunt and brusque, they should cultivate a sense of diplomacy and learn to respect the feeling of those with whom they are tossed.

When making a choice of mate for a marital type of relationship, the Sagittarian would be wise to settle on someone under the compatible signs of Aries or Leo— the least compatible signs would be for them, Pisces,

Gemini and Virgo. Of course, these are only indications—but the natives of the first two mentioned signs are naturally sympathetic to Sagittarius, and helpful. They should make excellent partners in business or bed. But definite rules cannot be laid down, and the best thing to do is find out all one can about one's own personality as indicated by the stars, then to do the same thing for the "other person."

The Sagittarian with his heavy Jupiter influence will probably succeed best as a banker, broker, manager, organizer, political worker, or any line where similar abilities are prerequisites for success. Sagittarius indicates that they should do well in sports, especially those dealing with dogs or horses.

They have excellent constitutions. "Strong as a horse." But they may be susceptible to symptoms of sciatica, gout or hip ailments. They should avoid rich or fried foods.

Their greatest success will come through a combination of their powers of intuition and their brilliant nature on something that will grab hold of their entire interest. They are capable of intense concentration, but if their concentration is interrupted, their interest is lost. By attaining this coordination and concentration their horizons are unlimited.

Those born between November 22nd
and December 2nd—

Are frank, open-hearted, and sincere natives of Sagittarius, who love to talk but are loathe to listen. When they speak it is the truth, and they expect the same from others. Duplicity is the one quality that makes them more irate than anything else when they discover it in another person. The symbol of their sign is the archer, and directness is their watchword.

They are of a philosophic turn of mind and their avocations reflect this. Their interests run to science, history and the humanities. As a vocation they would most likely excel as organizers or directors of large enterprises, or as financiers or statesmen.

Jupiter is the ruling planet of their sign and plays a most important part in their choice of a profession. He would most likely favor the native becoming a banker, lawyer, judge, clergyman, statesman or any of the professions of authority and power. He also smiles on merchants and woolen dealers, but makes for success in any line of work which the native may choose.

Mercury, the planet of the intellect was also dominant between these dates and lends its special influence to all those engaged in the production of literature: writers, editors, publishers, printers and booksellers. It also has a special influence over accountants, clerks, registrars, letter carriers, interpreters and teachers.

There are very few people who have a wide field of work from which to choose their life work. Their problem is to make a selection which is congenial to them. They would do best in a field where they can take plenty of vacations. Otherwise they might tend to plod. Plodding is not becoming to the centaur, and success does not come in that way to the Sagittarian.

The Sagittarians should go in for sports and games, all kinds. And they should be good at them, especially those that have something to do with horses or dogs. They don't usually have to be advised to get plenty of exercise in the open air, or to eat simply. It comes to them naturally. They do have to take care if symptoms show up that indicate ailments of the hips or thighs, or gout, or sciatica. Their constitutions are healthy even though their dispositions may be nervous.

The colors indicated by the planets for these children of Jupiter are blue, black, orange, slate, sea-green, violet and purple—and their flowers are goldenrod (beware all those who suffer from hay-fever). Their gems are turquoise, diamond, carbuncle, amethyst, emerald, sapphire, agate and marcasite. In order to dress in harmony with their stars they would wear any or all of the above (not at the same time, of course), but if they should find these colors, stones or flowers unbecoming to them it is not essential that they wear them.

Although their attribute of frankness is essentially a fine quality, it tends to get in the way of affairs of the heart. They are not naturally romantically inclined— they are much more direct. Jupiter, being the judge, inclines them to be more logical than emotional in choosing a mate. The little white lies necessary to keep many love affairs going are resented by the Sagittarian; he would prefer honesty to sparing a person's feelings. However, when he finds a person capable of understanding and appreciating him he makes a loyal and devoted other half.

Jupiter, the ruling planet of Sagittarius, presides over honor, glory, wealth and success, and the Sagittarius-born is especially fortunate also to be a child of Jupiter, the greater fortune. They inherit from him the qualities of benevolence, generosity, sincerity and spirituality. Although Jupiter is one of the strongest of influences in any horoscope, he too can suffer from afflictions and in such cases these attributes may be transmuted into extravagance, wastefulness and ostentatiousness, and the person so ruled may suffer loss as a result. The well-aspected Jupiter on the other hand greatly increases chances of good fortune, and frequently brings honors, spiritual enlightenment, worldly influence and gratified ambition.

Their intuition borders on clairvoyance, and they are handy people to have around in emergencies, especially when quick intuitive action is necessary, rather than slower logical action. Their flashes of insight and hunches are most generally correct and they do well to follow them. Their keen insight also gives them better information than most about what is going on in someone elses' mind—embarrassing sometimes!

Highly sensitive, yet not always considerate. Brusque and somewhat tactless. These are qualities that the Sagittarian must keep, but keep in check, less he end up with more enemies than friends. He has great qualities that can get him as far as he aims.

Those born between December 3rd
and December 12th—

Were born under the sign symbolized by the centaur, Sagittarius, and the planet Jupiter is the ruling planet of this sign. The Moon was a particularly dominant influence during this time, and this produces a most interesting and promising combination of influences. These influences would almost always be indicative of success, and if the people born with these aspects are not, it is most likely their own fault.

The planetary colors for these Sagittarians, due to the Moon's influence, tend to be somewhat lighter. They are white, pale yellow, pale green, flower is goldenrod and their gems are opal, moonstone, crystal, emerald, sapphire, amethyst, diamond, and topaz. They need not wear these stones, flowers and colors should they find them unbecoming, but if they wish to dress in harmony with the stars they will probably wear one or more of them from time to time.

In love this is the type of person who would most likely find a date at the midway of a carnival more to his liking than necking in a parked car. His theme song might well be "I only want a buddy, not a sweetheart," and this might be all right except that he wants so many buddies. This can lead to problems if he is not attached to someone who is in sympathy and understanding with his "problem."

Personal freedom is their dominant passion, and they may appear to have no soft side of their nature whatsoever. In love they are frequently as blunt and tactless as they are in their everyday relations.

Honors, position, success and wealth are theirs from Jupiter, and the dominant influence of the Moon translates these qualities in terms of the public. Jupiter lends its power for success to any line of work that the native may adopt, but is especially friendly to lawyers, bankers, judges, clergymen, statesmen and to all others in authority and power. They are naturally endowed and well fitted to organize and direct large enterprises, and may win fortune as a financier or a captain of industry.

The Moon favors public careers as well, and salesmen are among her favored sons (the traveling kind). She also governs over activities having to do with liquid and transportation, especially by water. Shipping, sailing and fishing and "those who go down (Ha!) to the sea in ships" come under her domain.

They are not lacking the variety of vocational fields that are open to them, but no matter which one they choose, they should, like the proud centaur that is the symbol of their sign, prance and not plod. Their inspirational flashes of intuition should serve to guide them far along the path to success, and they should have the ability easily to distinguish between impulse and insight.

Reflecting again the horsey part of their symbol, the centaur, they tend to be nervous, high-strung and over-sensitive. They wear their feelings, sometimes, on their sleeve, yet are extremely careless about how they treat those of other persons. And they don't always wait for a real slight to take offense—quite frequently they get their dander up over imaginary insults.

Patience to them would be a virtue if they had it. They all too often take up an enterprise with enthusiasm only to drop it before its completion. This type of thing can be frustrating to them as well as to others.

The Sagittarius-born must above all be a free soul. His natural exuberance and enthusiasm must be given free reign, else he turns unhappy and as stale as yesterday's champagne.

He should enjoy the best of health, and should not, nor is he likely to under (excuse the expression) normal circumstances, indulge in excesses of any sort. He should take care not to expose himself to infectious diseases, but even then he has splendid powers of recuperations and should throw off disease readily.

Those born between December 13th and December 21st—

Are born under the sign of Sagittarius, and their ruling planet is Jupiter. But Jupiter in this part of Sagittarius is modified and somewhat strengthened by the influence of Saturn, which was dominant in the heavens when these people were born. They are more of a serious nature than their fellow Sagittarians and have more of a sober temperament and philosophical turn of mind. They will be inclined toward research in both natural science and philosophy.

As do most Sagittarians, they have few friends, but the ones they have are close and loyal. In spite of their natural personal magnetism they have a brusqueness and lack of diplomacy that tends to turn people away from them. Their real nature, frequently hidden, is a gift from the frankness of Sagittarius along with his open-heartedness and from the genial humanity of Jupiter, and is most attractive. Consideration for others would show it off to its best advantage. They are highly sensitive, but tend to forget that other people are too.

Saturn has its influence in these natives in love and marriage and as well as being inherently loyal they are of an almost pure and chaste nature and resentful of licentiousness (whatever that is). They want to be appealed to on the mental and spiritual planes before they'll go to bed with you, or slip a band on your finger. They'll probably be more inclined to get married than to shack up.

Their colors are blue-green, blue, black, dark brown, purple, violet and indigo; and their flower (sneezers, beware) goldenrod. Along with all unpolished blue and black gems the planets favor diamond, topaz and lodestone for them. Should they find that these stones, flowers and colors do not become them it is not at all necessary that they wear them, but should they choose to include them in their wardrobe they will be dressing in harmony with their stars.

The disciplinary influence of Saturn over these people makes them less high-strung and nervous than others born under the sign of Sagittarius, and they have less excuse for suffering the real and imagined indignities of others, and less cause for hurting or estranging associates through their lack of tact or impulsive actions. They are capable of more concentration than most Sagittarians, and should make the most of their capabilities. They should not become bogged down in routine. They are not given to that type of operation. They should learn to finish one project before they go on to another, though, and through application can let their brilliance shine to its best advantage.

There is every indication that they should achieve success in literary or philosophic fields. Literature especially can be rewarding. More practical lines like banking, management, directing, organizing, finance and legislation are other fields in which they may excel.

Jupiter is likely to be the planet most involved in their choice of occupation, since it is their ruling planet, and he inclines his children to be bankers, lawyers, judges, clergymen, statesmen, and all such fields as require authority and power. Jupiter is broad minded, though, and lends his support to whatever line his children choose. Saturn governs more mundane activities and may incline the native to plumbing, undertaking, mining and fields dealing with coal or lead.

Most Sagittarians are natural athletes and should most certainly spend a goodly portion of their time in the out-of-doors. They should find any sport dealing with horses or dogs to their liking. They will most likely take good care of themselves, especially diet-wise, and have splendid constitutions. Attention should be paid, however, to any ailment that strikes at the hips or thighs, and to any signs of gout or sciatica.

Their instinct and intuition bestowed upon them by Jupiter is one of their best guides, and this, disciplined as it is by Saturn can be trusted.

CHAPTER TEN
CAPRICORN

DECEMBER 23RD
THROUGH JANUARY 20TH

Unromantic as it may sound, the Capricornians might well be called the goat-people. The goat is the symbol of their sign and they partake of many of the qualities of that animal. Sometimes the goat is represented as having the tail of a fish and to some extent they do have a double nature. For instance, they are inclined to be, as is the goat, capricious. This is hardly in harmony with another quality of the goat, that of cautiousness, but they have that quality, too. And, often to their detriment they are capricious and totally devoid of caution; and when it would best suit them to throw caution to the winds, is when they are most likely to exercise that characteristic.

Frequently they are old-men-before-their-time and considered to be overly cautious and lacking in sentiment. They do possess personal magnetism and charm, and tend to be fond of sex. When they express love, they want the nitty-gritty, and are very sudden and whimsical in their likes and dislikes. Their air of indifference often proves attractive to others, but the Capricornians never fall in love until they are absolutely sure of reciprocation.

On occasion they will make alliances which appear to be most enduring and powerful; but, if they feel that their pride has been hurt they can turn on an icy indifference that would freeze over the Sahara. They are an earthy lot and place a great deal of stock on worldly advantage, and are exciting and jealous in their relations with their loved ones. Their own happiness and popularity could be much greater were they to be more unselfish toward others, and if they would stimulate their more tender emotions.

They are willing to plod along step after step, testing the ground as it were; and this, with natural inclination to be industrious, their instinct for accuracy, and their unceasing ambition to rise to the top and get ahead, generally enables the Capricornians to make a financial success of their lives.

Frequently they find that their natural application can find its best rewards in the fields of manufacturing, wholesale clothing, building and architecture, realty, mining, agriculture and forestry. Another, specially educated type of Capricorn-born person exists that will most likely find better expression if they become educators, biologists (by the Braille system?), politicians, public speakers and historians.

The Capricornian by virtue of his sign suffers quite frequently from a feeling of dependency upon other people, and they should, if at all possible, prepare themselves early in life to meet any emergency by being prepared to do some sort of constructive work that will enable them to earn their own living—even if all prospects show that it will never be necessary for them to do so.

They have the continual tendency to take upon themselves the responsibility of the destiny of other people, usually an error on their part. They do not bear in mind that it is best for all concerned to let each person work out his own destiny and that there is little they can do toward the salvation of others. Everyone in this day and age especially, either knowingly or unknowingly is trying to be financially independent and economically free.

Even though the Capricorn-born are natural workers and as such frequently find themselves in the service of others, they are never servile. They have no need to ask the way for they have what might be called an inborn sense of direction, much as have the migrating birds. They step cautiously, but deliberately and find their own way. Capable people all, they make their own way. They are excellent planners and can make a budget work. (Something a lot of us can't do!) They are seldom pinch-pennies, but late in life they may fall into regrets and become exceedingly parsimonious. It might be well to take one on a shopping trip too, since they have the reputation of being able to drive a sharp bargain. They have no pipe dreams, and are very practical. They are much too cautious to ever be called visionaries, and have the habit of carefully testing new ground before they tread thereupon.

Those born most strongly under the influence of the ruling planet of this sign, Saturn, have a tendency toward despondency and melancholy. They worry and fret about the future and are always saving up for that rainy day, and could never take to heart the meaning of the phrase, "Consider the lilies of the field...." They are sure that they are the one sparrow that God doesn't have his eye on.

Even though the obstacles that they frequently find in their path would seem insurmountable to most people, the Capricorn, with the agility of the symbol of his sign, the goat, uses these very obstacles as stepping stones to scale the heights and achieve his goal, their caution and industry aiding them every step and leap of the way. Supremacy in the political world is a distinction sought by many men of this sign. The rewards of a work are of most concern to them, and they seldom do anything just for the love of doing it. They are leaders and organizers, and if an undertaking is incidental to their ultimate goal they can take it on, no matter how overwhelming it might be, and succeed where most would fail.

Their thirst for knowledge is almost insatiable, and they gain a great deal of information and wisdom through experience. They respect and admire those who are more experienced and knowledgeable than they, but all too frequently are misled into believing that rote knowledge can be equated with wisdom.

There are times when the Capricorn person seems to be absolutely motionless as far as progress is concerned. These are his times of deliberation, and as long as he remains awake he can well afford them. He is entitled to slow down from time to time for when he's in action (wow!) he's direct and swift.

The native of this sign loves to travel, and on his journeys frequently runs into people who are anxious to help him on his way up. Sometimes though, their ambition and determination become so obvious that it is obnoxious, and they incur the enmity of their higher ups, and the jealousy of those lower in the social scale than they because of their success.

Those Capricorns who are less developed (not that way, girl) are: self-assertive, selfish, suspicious, head-strong, and have great extremes of mood and temper. Saturn supplies them with no natural levity, and they oftentimes resort to the use of alcohol or drugs as a crutch. Your secret drinkers are frequently Capricorn-born. While other people are social drinkers, the Capricorn uses it as a mental or physical stimulant. This tendency can be overdone.

Although they have many natural abilities, the Capricornians do not always have the necessary faith in their abilities. They should make use of these abilities and the present time, for upon this their future depends. They worry too frequently about that which will never happen, and find themselves too often engrossed in crossing bridges that they have not yet reached.

Those born between December 22nd
and January 1st—

Are born under the sign of the goat, the sign of Capricorn. Their ruling planet is that great disciplinarian Saturn, and the dominant planet at the time of their birth was Jupiter.

Consistent with the symbol of their sign, the goat, the Capricorn-born is continually striving to reach the heights of his ambition, and overcome all obstacles in his path by persistence, endurance and his consuming ambition.

The natives of this sign hold fast to that which they have and attach a great importance to the marital state. Sometimes though they may find it difficult to use the finesse necessary to make a successful one. Seldom do those born under this earthy sign confine their affections to a spiritual plane, and they are subject to whims and whimsy. Such activity frequently leads to mudslinging, with the Capricorn the recipient of the facial.

They tend to be all too self-centered in love. They have little or no sympathy for children (but that shouldn't bother most of the readers of this book). In love, it is unfortunate, they are all too often their own worst enemies.

If they wish to dress in harmony with their stars the planets indicate that their colors are ash-gray, green, black, brown (a favorite of theirs, I've heard), maroon, purple, violet and indigo. Their flowers are the poppy, flax and holly; and their jewels: onyx, moss agate, garnet, lodestone, emerald, sapphire and amethyst. If they find these not to their liking it's no great hang-up.

They are possessed of industry, perseverance and caution. One might even say that they are possessed by caution. In spite of the broadmindedness that could be theirs as children of Jupiter, they are doubting Thomases, and frequently become overly fearful of the outcome of things and have a dread of impending failure. The success of a Capricorn person usually arrives late in life.

This part of Capricorn tends to make its natives very orthodox in their attitude toward religion, and they often become strict disciplinarians of themselves, almost martyrs. They are domestically oriented and love great gatherings of the clan and the celebrations of birthdays, anniversaries, too. They especially enjoy being hosts at these affairs.

Ambition which gives incentive and initiative, and followed through by industry and hard work invariably leads to success. Many statesmen are born under this sign, which lends it subjects all of these attributes. They are also proficient as manufacturers, builders, miners, foresters and realtors.

Saturn, that old kill-joy disciplinarian, indicates that they can also succeed by the sweat of their brow in such occupations as plumbing (look at Josephine), undertaking, mining and dealing in lead or coal.

Jupiter gives a girl a better chance and governs judges, lawyers, bankers, clergymen, statesmen and all in power and authority. Jupiter is also friendly to woolen dealers (wolves in sheep's clothing) and provision dealers. But best of all, Jupiter smiles on almost every line of endeavor and leaves the field wide open.

True sons of Capricorn have iron constitutions and have no fear except for their digestive tract. Keep the Alka-Seltzer handy, and drink lotsa water. They're going to have to do a lot of hard work, but they've got the physical power to do it with.

Those born between January 2nd and January 11th—

Are ambitious, purposeful and industrous as indicated by the sign of Capricorn under which they were born. Mars was dominant in the heavens when they were born and gives them added energy, initiative, enthusiasm and aggressiveness, so all indications of the sign are doubly applied to those born between these dates. If they can moderate their warlike and quarrelsome tendencies they should gain both honor and fame.

It could be said that their symbol should be the ant rather than the goat (no insult implied or otherwise) since they are born workers. They are tireless and possessed of an insatiable ambition. They hunger for power, and seek the knowledge and wealth that they know will give it to them. They attract influential friends (or should we say 'make them?'). They make sure they get their share of favors, and though surrounded by rivals, they never come out second best.

Sometimes their concern and brooding over the future makes them unwilling to enjoy the present to the fullest and they appear to be taking life too seriously.

The colors for these remarkable people are green, black, dark brown, blood red, scarlet, blue green, ash-gray and indigo. Their gems according to the planets are moon crystal, onyx, garnet and lodestone. Their flowers? Poppy, holly and flax. To dress in harmony with their planetary influences they may wear any or all of the above, but if their sense of decoration indicates that these are unbecoming to their drag they can leave them all off and have a ball.

The love nature of the Capricorn is not satisfied unless it has a husband and a home. Home ownership, or at least having command of a home is one of their goals, but once attained they can be overbearing with those with whom they share it.

They are persistent and tenacious, and have the striking characteristic of being able to surmount almost all difficulties that come in their way while on their way to the top. They're sure there's room there—if not they'll make it. Even when they've scaled the peaks of their ambition they look for further 'up' to go.

They should choose occupations in which these gifts are of prime import such as mining, farming, manufacturing, building, planning. Any occupation that requires tireless, unending effort can be tackled by them, and they might find success in statesmanship and military affairs (both kinds).

Saturn, on the other hand, indicates a more mundane type of occupation, and Saturn is their ruling planet.

He favors such things as plumbing, mining, under-taking (deadly thought) and coal and lead dealing. He is a disciplinarian, and as such favors most occupations which require a great deal of brawn and sweat of the brow.

Mars, the planet dominant at the time of the birth of these people lends a spirit of initiative, courage and executive ability to them, and will help them in any line where these attributes are requisites of success. He is particularly influential in all matters pertaining to soldiers, surgeons, chemists, dentists, barbers and other workers with sharp instruments (critics?) or with iron or steel or fire.

All of the cardinal signs, Capricorn, Aries, Cancer and Libra have to give the greatest attention to their digestive systems and must be particularly careful in the selections of their diets and to any problems that might arise in elimination.

Capricorns are in particular susceptible to inflammatory conditions, especially those rheumatic in nature. Their tendency to brood on their troubles, real or imagined, could easily bring on an intestinal imbalance resulting in dyspepsia or severe headaches. Too much of this could interfere with their success. Association with cheerful people is the best medicine for them. They need cheering up because of their heavy Saturn influence.

Those born between January 12th
and January 20th—

Have: ambition, patience, tenacity, industry; all excellent qualities of the Capricorn goat. These are qualities which enable the Capricorn-born to overcome obstacles, and are prominent in most of the persons born under this forceful, purposeful sign.

The natives of this sign have a tendency toward melancholy; a direct result of the sobering influence of the great heavenly disciplinarian Saturn, the ruler of this sign. All too frequently the Capricornian is cold and austere, and lacking in sympathy and grace. They tend to be introverted and wrapped up in their own interests. Their struggle against coldness and pride may not be easy.

Although at heart they are jealous and demanding lovers and strongly swayed by their emotions, they too often appear to be overly practical and unsentimental.

The Capricorn person will most likely find the best marriage partner born under either the sign of Taurus or Virgo; these signs being of the earth triplicity and the most helpful and sympathetic to the Capricorn. On the other hand alliances with Aries, Cancer or Libra would most likely turn out to be misalliances. However, it is impossible to predict the outcome of any relationship between two persons without complete astrological data on both parties concerned.

The colors best suited to the Capricorn born between these dates are yellow, yellow-brown, gold, orange, green, ash-gray, maroon, dark brown and black. Their planetary flowers are holly, flax and the poppy. Their best gems are chrysolite, lode-stone, garnet and all unpolished black and blue stones.

When working hardest the Capricorn-born is at his best and is happiest. The gifts bestowed upon them by the stars are practical ones, and they should make use of them. They are well suited by their energy and perseverance to attain the goals in all constructive applications, especially those where the chief requisite is hard work. These include building, manufacturing, mining and farming.

Probably the most influential factor in the determination of their choice of occupation will be the influence of the planet Saturn which is the ruling planet of Capricorn. Saturn is a most practical planet and lends his support toward success to all fields of endeavor which require strenuous effort. He favors especially such occupations as plumbing, undertaking (how moribund!), mining or dealing in coal or lead.

The Sun was dominant in the heavens when these particular Capricornians were born and he tends to favor all those who are in places of authority and involved in statesmanship or commerce. He is also favorable to jewelers and all others dealing with or working in precious metals. The children of this sign do have a very wide field from which to choose their life's work, and may succeed once they learn application, in any of them. But it is important that they choose one that is most congenial to them.

At times they may feel that their progress is exceedingly slow, and indeed it may be, almost discouragingly so. They will find life itself a difficult struggle at times. Saturn, their ruling planet, is never in any great hurry, and is a very strict teacher, making sure that every lesson is learned well. He does allow success eventually, although sometimes not until very late in life. He is for their eventual success, although at times it may seem as if he is very much opposed.

Even the objective observer of the Capricorn person may think that he is standing still. This too is the trait of the goat, who frequently stands absolutely still contemplating his next leap. Like the goat, the native of this sign travels in spurts. They do not progress steadily or quickly to their goal, but, what's more important, they do progress, and with the application they have, they do reach it.

The besetting sin of the Capricornian all too frequently is that of worrying, too often about that which will never happen; and second to that, the one of hesitating too long before taking action. They are equipped (wow!) for success and should use (frequently) their equipment to full advantage.

Worry is their greatest enemy, and may lead to actual physical disorders if indulged in too frequently or too long. They should guard against this tendency, especially when it develops rheumatic tendencies and digestive upsets. They should in their diets stick to the simple foods, and drink plenty of water. But above all, they should try to adopt a cheerful outlook on life.

CHAPTER ELEVEN
AQUARIUS

JANUARY 21ST THROUGH FEBRUARY 19TH

The list of the Aquarius-born who have risen to great heights is a long one. Fully eighty percent of those enshrined in the nation's Hall of Fame were born under this sign. Names recently in the news that are famous (although sometimes, and let's be honest, infamous) Aquarians are: Eddie Arcaro, Omar N. Bradley, Cassius Clay, Everett M. Dirksen, John Dos Passos, Norman Mailer, Harold R. Medina, James A. Michener, Louis Nizer, S. J. Pearlman, Bishop James A. Pike, Admiral Hyman Rickover, Norman Rockwell, Abraham Lincoln. And just to be fair, let's add: Thomas Edison, Franklin D. Roosevelt, and Havelock Ellis.

The symbol of this sign of Aquarius is called the waterbearer, but is usually represented by a man pouring out water. This latter is more indicative of the general nature of the sign, which is out-giving. The natives of this sign are usually great humanitarians and they live most generally for the good of others. And they give of themselves, and as so frequently happens those who give receive, and so do they. In turn for their outpouring of themselves they frequently receive the reward of fame.

Although Aquarius is in reality an air sign it is frequently thought of, by association, as a water sign—but once it is understood that this water which in its symbol is being poured out is representative of the water of life, the relationship between it and the breath of life can easily be seen.

We won't even mention the staff of life. Everybody knows about that.

The Aquarian native has the ability to inspire people, both through their ability to lead and through their ability to set an example. They are usually noted for being gentle and helpful, and are kind-hearted people. They are most happy when their advice is sought, and are usually good advisors. They are most immediately influenced, however, by their immediate surroundings, and their concern is for the person nearest to them at the present moment. They are subject to being taken advantage of, not through flattery as are the children of other signs, but through the fault of their own natural sympathetic nature. Frequently the sacrifices that they make are not fully appreciated, and they must learn to show discrimination in the dispensation of their favors, and not allow their tolerance to blind them to the fact that they sometimes are being taken without their knowing it.

They are often overlooked as a result of their modesty and lack of presumption, but rarely does this bother them. They are born people-watchers, and delight in observing the interactions of society in the world about them. All too frequently this trait sets them off from other persons in what might be called their own private isolation booth. They tend to be rather quiet and reserved. Others then find them difficult to approach, and attempts to penetrate their exterior are thwarted (sob!). Their underlying abilities are frequently unobserved, and like the power of the woman, underestimated.

The developed Aquarian, however is highly intellectual. They may well be looked to as the possible mentors of the coming age. The Aquarian native would do quite well to live as he is inclined, from moment to moment, from place to place, completely in the here and now, taking full advantage of every situation as it presents itself to him.

All too frequently the native of Aquarius lacks sufficient confidence in his own mental and spiritual powers, then as a result of his desire to be of service (don't we all?) he all too willingly takes the advice of others against his own better judgment and intuition. The greatest mistakes and misfortune that befall the Aquarian are likely to come through such misguidance.

Persons born under this humanitarian sign are usually very even-tempered, and only after quiet deliberation do they take offense at anything, and then only if it appears to them to be unjust or petty. Their environment seldom has power over them as a result of their extreme mental poise. They are almost always equal to their circumstances, no matter what they are and no matter where they be. The Aquarian is a determined individual, and when he has envisioned a plan, he holds fast to his vision and goes about to accomplish its fulfillment and develop it at the first opportunity.

The children of this sign are remarkably free from prejudice, and as far as they are concerned, nothing they conceive of is impossible of accomplishment. They are open-minded to all concepts and will accept facts which seem to be diametrically opposed to all of their theories; then, after careful analysis, if they find this new information of value to their purpose, they set about at once to incorporate it into their plans and thereby reap the good attainable from such incorporation.

Empirical knowledge comes easily to them, but by the same token, they can never be trusted to remember such trivia as names, addresses and phone numbers. Better write it down for them, then hope that they'll call. They do forget things like that, too. Fact, they never forget. They may not remember who or when or where, but they'll always remember what and how and why.

They are not great ones for putting themselves forward, and when they do it is usually for the purpose of solving a situation for someone else. The simplicity with which they solve many situations never ceases to be a source of wonder to their friends and associates, especially since they never seem to have been paying any attention at all to what had been going on.

The nature of the Aquarian is to aim for that which is humanitarian, universal, impersonal and helpful. Their love and devotion is for all humanity, and this they continually pour out rather than concentration on themselves or upon purely personal relationships. (Often to the consternation of those near to them, who would prefer a more personal relationship.) They are great reformers, but more of the revolutionary type and not the let's-go-back-to-the-good-old-days kind; and in these reformation endeavors they usually plan more work for themselves than can ever reasonably hope to accomplish. The results they are seeking are also sometimes delayed by their own impulsive natures.

Their logical minds give them great powers not only of deduction, but of inductive reasoning as well. Once a person has granted them the validity of their first premise, they are able to proceed and convince their listener by their acute powers of reasoning, which is greatly enhanced by their ability to illustrate their contention by the most charming and convincing smiles they possess.

Although they are very personable people, in their affairs of the heart they tend to be somewhat impersonal, and if ever out-of-sight-out-of-mind could be applied to an individual, it could be called the theme song of the Aquarian. He is more wrapped up in his immediate environment, wherever that may be, and the people in his immediate vicinity, whomsoever they may be, and for the moment forgets individual loyalties.

He is not possessive and does not know what possession is. However, if the Aquarian intends to direct himself to any one individual in a personal relationship, he would do best to seek a partner in the airy signs of Gemini or Libra, these signs having a greater understanding of him than any other. In order to determine the degree of success of any such relationship, however, it would be necessary to have not only the month and day of birth of both parties concerned, but the year and place, and if at all possible the hour and minute as well, so that complete horoscopes for both parties could be cast and thereby a better judgment formed.

The sign of Aquarius rules, in the physical body, the legs, ankles, teeth and the circulatory system, and also to some extent the heart and the throat. Those born under this sign, although quite active on the mental and spiritual planes, are not prone to engage in active sports or bodily exercise. Frequently this lack of activity leads to such ailments or disorders as poor circulation of the blood and poor elimination. Rheumatism or mild blood poisoning may be symptoms which plague them from time to time. Their tendency toward a sedentary, almost inert existence may make them subject to attacks of constipation.

They should force themselves into some sort of physical activity (or maybe someone could entice them into it) and see that they get plenty of fresh air and rest. They will tend to eat a simple diet, if indeed they remember to eat at all, which is good. Too often, though they do forget to eat and become undernourished.

Lack of exercise combined with an inadequate diet may lead them into a weakened condition which would make them more liable to infection. The first symptoms they would be liable to notice would be a tendency toward fatigue and/or insomnia. They of all people should have a competent physician. Frequently their infections are of the teeth or the tonsils.

The poor circulation of the Aquarian makes him more prone to feel the cold than most people. And they have the coldest feet of all. Scratches or cuts should be taken care of immediately and they should avoid living in zones where blood-carried diseases predominate.

Those people born under the sign of Aquarius are able to be most constructive in nearly every facet of living because of their unusual sense of human understanding and the great adaptability with which their sign has endowed them. Financially they can, for this very reason, make a success of their lives in almost any field which they choose for themselves, or in which they find themselves—it makes little difference.

Financial reward, however, is actually the least of their concerns; their main esteem for money being that they consider it only as a means to an end. Frequently their endeavors prove more financially beneficial to others than to themselves. They are not shrewd or conniving enough to be in business for themselves, and should not be, unless they are engaged in one of the professions and cannot do otherwise.

They need to be needed, and have to feel it. Unless they are helping humanity or raising the status of the underdog they are not happy, and the simple act of making money is not sufficient incentive for them to make a go of any type of commercial venture. Their inventive and constructive talents would be in most cases wasted in the more mundane business fields.

The Aquarian might well be compared to the immovable object. Even though he may find himself surrounded by and acted upon from all sides by irresistible forces, he remains calm, cool and collected. His control comes from within. There is probably no other sign that has as natives so large a group of people so near to self-mastery.

Those born between January 21st
and January 30th—

Were born under the sign symbolized by the water-bearer, the sign of Aquarius. The planet of the god of invention (and by name associated with the goddess of spiritual love), Uranus (pronounced: your anus) is the ruling planet of this sign.

Basically then, the through-and-through Aquarian son is a humanitarian, and they give of themselves to humanity. They look objectively at things not only from an overall mundane standpoint, but form a higher cosmic standpoint as well. Theirs is a universal love, not a personal one. They will embrace ideals, studies and institutions of mercy before they will an individual. Bluntly speaking, they spread themselves all over the place.

This tendency for concentration on an individual puts them in the position of making friends very slowly (if they even get around to it), but if their associates can stand the test of time the Aquarian will be a dedicated and loyal friend, and the best kind to have in time of trouble.

There is little of the materialistic or physical nature in their makeup, and consistent with their being an air sign they will more often be of a spiritual or mental bent. Self-control is probably easier for them than for any of the other signs of the Zodiac, and once having attained it, they will reflect a virtually endless patience-of-a-saint, tremendous power of concentration and an unearthly mental poise. This latter is among their finest characteristics.

They are insistent on meeting all people on their own mental plane, and it is their right so to do. Their only intention is the upliftment of others, but unfortunately others frequently mistake it for ostentation and snobbery. Spiritual discussions do not lead to quick tricks. They do have the capability though of engendering a feeling of popularity with everybody, but all at the same time. And this tendency to broadcast affections can engender misunderstandings concerning the placement of individual loyalty and devotion.

The planets indicate a goodly variety of flowers, colors and gems for them to wear, and if they wish to dress in harmony with their stars they can include whatever ones they wish to in their wardrobe. If they find any or all of them unsuitable or unbecoming, however, they may without consequence omit them. The colors indicated are light blue, bluish green and ultramarine. Their flowers are (and let's all watch and see how many of them wear these) the tulip, the daffodil and (are you ready?) the pansy. The jewels indicated for them are opal, sapphire, beryl, green jasper, lapis-lazuli and carnelian.

Physically speaking the typical son of Aquarius is not a strong person. They should be on their guard against such ailments as poor circulation, gout, cramps and rheumatism. They should encourage proper elimination (a good douche might help now and then) and avoid chills (personally, next to my own skin I like the feeling of skin best). They should take especial care of their legs and feet. (My doctor tells me that to stimulate circulation in the lower extremities leg raises are the best exercise.)

The most influential planet of course, in directing the Aquarian toward a profession, is the ruling planet of the sign, Uranus. This plane governs lecturers, public officials, engineers (especially those along electronic lines), mechanics (telephone installers and TV men), and all those who pursue the more uncommon professions such as astrologers, psychologists and metaphysicians.

Venus, planet of love, was also dominant at the time these people were born and may incline them to other fields. She rules musicians, poets, actors, painters, artists of all kinds, dealers in perfumes, flowers, ornaments and toilet articles and accessories, silk merchants, embroiders, makers of hats, gloves, women's apparel and other drag, fancy goods dealers, bakers and confectioners.

Venus also lends support for successful ventures into the lighter sciences and the fine arts. Aquarians generally can succeed in any endeavor which is dedicated to the advancement of humanity such as teaching, medicine and social work, but these particular Aquarians with the added benefits heaped upon them by Venus can do well also in such specialized trades as writers, decorative artists or entertainers.

They are tenacious to their ideals, and their ideals are humanitarian. Their greatest delight is derived from their successful efforts to help others, and their greatest threat and danger arises out of this in that they are liable to place entirely too much trust in human nature, assuming it to be too much like their own. Even though affairs are in a constant state of flux about them, and try to push them hither and yon, once their mind is made up, they stand steadfast until they finally see the accomplishment of their goals.

Those born between January 31st
and February 9th—

Astrologically speaking children of Aquarius, born in one of the best and most favored signs of the Zodiac, and in the most fortunate parts of that sign. The planet which controls the intellect, Mercury, was the dominant planet in the heavens at the time of their birth.

The typical son of Aquarius is by his very nature inclined to be a great humanitarian. His greatest pleasure is to do good unto others, with little or no concern about what others are doing unto him. They see the broader aspect of the whole world. Rising above their own personal desires and above the selfish aims of most they take the cosmic view. These people born between the dates of January 31st and February 9th have all these traits and abilities of the Aquarian, plus the added special influence of Mercury, who gives them the ability to make use of these traits to their best advantage.

In order to dress in harmony with their stars they may wear any or all of the flowers, jewels or colors indicated for them by the planetary influences at the time they were born. The colors so indicated are blue, bluish green and black. The flower children among them will most likely bedeck themselves with primroses, pansies and daffodils. And in their jewelry they would do well to include some things fashioned out of agate, marcasite, emerald, topaz, opal and sapphire. If on the other hand they would, for some reason prefer not to wear any or all of the above, little or nothing would be lost by the decision. Especially in the case of the pansy.

Caution is advised to the Aquarian in love. Although he is basically devoted and loyal he is inclined not to be demonstrative. His interest lies in the world, is general all too often to the neglect of the person who should be first in his affections. This attitude just doesn't set well with most men. They like to feel important—and the Aquarian who has set up housekeeping with them would do quite well to bear this in mind, and while at home, at least, suppress his broadcasting of love and do a command performance for one.

The entire field of metaphysics, astrology included is ruled by Uranus, which is the governing planet of the sign of Aquarius, and the planet most like to have an influence in the Aquarians choice of profession. Its favorable influence is extended also to lecturers, public officials, travelers, electricians and all dealers in scientific equipment.

Mercury, the planet which governs the intellect, and the one dominant in the heavens at the time of birth of these sons of Aquarius, governs, on the other hand, writers, teachers, booksellers, publishers, printers, editors, accountants, interpreters, registrars, clerks and letter carriers. Those born under these influences might even excel as physicians, social workers and inventors, and some may even become interested in astronomy, astrology and research into matters occult.

These native of Aquarius never become bogged down because of laziness or changeability. They work hard, and they work until the work is done. They are seldom known to be overnight successes. Their success is won only after long and hard work, and sometimes after many failures. When fame comes to them, however, it is a lasting fame. The example of two famous Aquarians points to that: Abraham Lincoln and Thomas Alva Edison.

They see beyond money as an end in itself, and see through to the symbol of what it stands for and what it can do. It is a means to an end. The knowledge that they have helped someone to get more out of life means more to them than any monetary reward they might receive. And if they are true to their sign, they will receive this reward, perhaps many times—and may even make the monetary gains as well.

Aquarians born between these dates are slightly sturdier than are their brothers on both sides of them, and have a richer endowment mentally as well. They have an insight that is just this side of clairvoyance, and indeed, with practice they might develop this sense as well. Their health is for the most part good, and properly guarded they should experience relatively little poor health. They should watch their tendency to neglect their diet however, and keep their organs and glands functioning.

Generally they will enjoy a good reputation—they seldom do anything to make it otherwise. (But it's so much fun, they really should try). They are loyal, and once they dedicate themselves their self-sacrifices in devotion knows no end. But ideals, and not individuals are the usual recipients of this loyalty, service and devotion. Their generous nature to over-give of themselves can prove to be their own undoing, and this they should guard against.

*Those born between February 10th
and February 19th—*

Were born under the most optimistic sign of the Zodiac, the sign of Aquarius. The dark cloudy Moon, however, was dominant in the heavens when these people were born and is likely to shade the natural optimism and cheerfulness of them.

However, the more typical sons of Aquarius will concentrate on the prime purpose and dedication of the natives of this sign to the upliftment of humanity, and this will in turn keep their mind off any troubles, real or imagined, of their own.

The only slight that really ever affects the Aquarian native is the feelings that a person or persons are ungrateful for his efforts and he then might feel despondent and discouraged over the apparent hopelessness of human nature, and as a result lessen his efforts of well-doing. Generally their compensation for their efforts comes from unexpected sources, and seldom from those who have been the direct beneficiaries.

If the Aquarian is wearing pansies and daffodils he is wearing flowers in harmony with his stars (although I doubt if you'll ever see such decorations on them), and if he wants to go all the way and wear the jewels and colors that are indicated by the planetary vibrations, the colors indicated are blue, bluish green, pale yellow, pale green and white. His jewels are crystal, moonstone, opal and sapphire. If his better judgment tells him that any of these flowers, gems or colors are unsuited or unbecoming he might be better off not wearing them.

All people born under the sign of Aquarius succeed best in some profession or business which is dedicated to the service of mankind, and they frequently enter the fields of medicine, social service, invention and the promotion of the larger philanthropic enterprises.

The most influential factor, planetwise, will be Uranus, the ruling planet of their sign. Uranus governs the entire field of metaphysics and may lead its children to follow the lines of astrology, psychology and all related fields. It does express special concern where inventors, engineers, public officials, lecturers, electricians and dealers in scientific equipment are involved.

The Moon, the other planet dominant in the heavens at the time of their birth, favors all activities that have to do with the sea (and sailors). These Aquarians might make good sailors or shipping merchants. Import and export are fields open to them. They may enjoy traffic in liquids.

The Moon's strong influence in their horoscope may also give them a kind of wanderlust which will lead them to travel in foreign lands, and unless they're watchful this love for newer vistas may keep them too long from their real purpose in life. They may tend to have rather strange tastes and voracious appetites, and like a famous actress express a desire to be alone.

With the strange influences of the Moon combined with the subtle influences of their ruler Uranus, these people do not mix as well as most Aquarians. They should.

In love they tend not to be demonstrative, and give the uncertain feeling to their other half that he is neglected. In this field, it is especially necessary that they come outside of themselves and let their inner feelings express themselves to the fullest.

Eventually, when they learn to overcome the dark influences of their Moon, they will burst forth, radiant in all their glory. Then, letting their inventive powers vent their full expression, gain their just rewards.

CHAPTER TWELVE
PISCES

FEBRUARY 20TH THROUGH MARCH 20TH

The twelfth and last sign of the Zodiac is Pisces, and it rules the period between February 20th through March 20th. It is the third sign of the water triplicity, and has as a symbol two fishes, one swimming upstream and the other swimming downstream—a symbol most appropriate to its aquatic nature. We have observed other double signs; the twins of Gemini traveling two roads to the same goal, the scorpion and eagle of Scorpio expressing the wide range of possibilities for the sign, the centaur of Saggitarius indicating the transmutation of feelings, the fish-goat of Capricorn pointing out both its speed and its hesitancy. And here we again have a double sign, a double-natured sign, one fish struggling against the flow of the stream and the other drifting with the tide.

The Pisceans are honest in their intent and expect to find honesty in return. They walk on the sunny side of the street and look for the silver lining. They gullibly believe almost all that they hear. Generosity is their besetting virtue, and are frequently guilty of giving the shirts off their back. Lovers both of beauty and nature they see the good and ignore that which they find displeasing.

In their desire to help other people they often deplete their own resources. They seldom use judgment in their giving as do the Aquarians, and seem only to be bothered by the fact that they cannot give more. Unlike the more selfish signs, they do not consider anyone to whom they have given 'beholden' to them, and seldom if ever ask for an accounting.

On the other hand, they love to talk. And they love especially to talk about the things that they have done for other people, and verbally to make martyrs of themselves. Frequently they fall into the habit of self-pity. In this their unselfishness becomes a type of selfishness in itself. Sometimes they even go so far as to force their aid or assistance on others when it is neither wanted nor welcome. Their delight is in the assumption of responsibility, and usually they can be depended upon.

The typical Piscean is not an egotist, and frequently is found deficient in self-esteem. They are not always quitters, but they frequently feel of small consequence and see no reason for trying to keep pace with the world around them. Religious they are, but their religion is their own, and sometimes rather strange to other people. Regarding the law, they respect the spirit but do not always adhere to the letter of it.

Their nervousness and enthusiasm often calls attention to their undirected activity even in spite of their inclination to be modest and retiring. When they worry they exaggerate, and lend their anxiety to happenings and accidents that are most likely not to happen. They can weaken themselves physically by their frenzied fancies.

They are optimists, one time failing to recognize any or all obstacles in their paths and tending to under-estimate the length of time necessary to complete a task; then pessimists, jousting at windmills and fret if all does not go just according to plan.

They tend also to be somewhat scatter-brained or absent-minded and are constantly leaving things behind them and forgetting to pick them up (or bring them back). They are intuitive and impressionable, but lacking in logic and consistency. Sometimes they are very trying and stubborn as a result. They are as quick to let go of ideas as they are to latch on to them, unless their stubborn nature is aroused.

If the Piscean learns to recognize, then overcomes his inherent weaknesses he is a most delightful companion and lover. Even though they are loyal and devoted and generous to a fault, even toward those opposing them, few ever get through to their real love nature.

They are often disappointed in love when they find that few are willing to make the sacrifices that they themselves make—sometimes to the point of finding their associates selfish inasmuch as their apparent selflessness is taken for granted and neither appreci-ated nor reciprocated. If they were a bit more subtle in expressing their affections, a bit less demonstrative, perhaps, they might find greater acceptance.

When they are choosing their lovers they might do well to search out persons born under one of the other water signs, either Cancer or Scorpio, since these signs are the most sympathetic and helpful to Pisces. They would probably do well to avoid any lengthy alliances with those born under the signs of Gemini, Virgo or Saggitarius. In any case the success of an alliance such as this can only be predicated upon a comparison of the complete horoscope of both individuals involved.

At times the native of Pisces is a great talker, and appears to know a great deal more about the subject at hand than he actually does—and at others he has nothing to say. This alternate tendency to be loquacious or taciturn largely depends upon the people with whom he is associating at the time. Naturally confident they tend to speak openly, but once deceived they become suspicious and secretive. Often they assimilate and digest information on a subconscious level and bring forward truths of which they were not aware.

Like Alice with her mushroom, they are either up, or down; brilliant, cheerful and witty at one time; inert, peevish and melancholy at another. They are very sensitive by the nature of their sign and can become easily discontent and unhappy if they associate too long with the worldly materialistic.

"Oh, I think that's funny; that's so funny!" could be a phrase frequently falling from the lips of the Piscean individual. They have an uncanny knack for seeing the ridiculous side of almost any situation—unfortunately their laughter is sometimes deemed mockery by their associates and as such, hurts. For this reason, and others they are often misjudged and mistrusted.

The Piscean is a restless person—fidgety one might say, and often inattentive to what is being said. Even in their rare moments of outward calm, they are inwardly quaking.

They do not work well alone, and in business need to be associated with an organization, persons or person that can supply the necessary strength to bring about success. Though lacking somewhat in self-confidence, they are conscientious and as such make good partners. If they are developed and educated they may succeed as writers and painters, and their work reflects the bright side of their nature.

They tend to lack method and order in their personal affairs and are generally lousy housekeepers, even though they may be immaculate in their personal appearance. They may find gratification in any occupation which calls upon them to give unstintingly of themselves, such as nursing.

Those born between February 20th
and February 29th—

Have Neptune, the inspirational planet as their guiding star, and he rules over their astrological sign of Pisces, often called the birth sign of poets, artists, and dreamers. This sign is represented by two fishes, one swimming upstream and the other downstream. In this symbol one can see both their strength and their weakness.

Generally, the Piscean partakes of good health, but must take care against catching colds. Such respiratory ailments may affect the chest or the abdomen. Self-indulgence is a weakness of the sons of Pisces and they would do well to avoid excesses in drugs and alcohol.

Being children of a water sign and ruled by the king of the sea they should do well in lines having to do with liquids, as well as those other fields which Neptune governs in the artistic, aesthetic and inspirational realms. They should also make good teachers, social workers or imaginative writers, and might even find success in the theater or motion picture industry.

They have an unorthodox sense of religion, and if they let it dominate them may even tend to fanaticism. Their enthusiasm may become unhealthy due to the influence of Saturn at the time when they were born. Their reputations may come under attack from false friends or powerful enemies.

Saturn, their dominant planet, governs miners, plumbers and realtors, and may lead them into a similar field—or perchance into some other equally practical way of life.

They do love change, and resent the responsibility of a home and family. If they ever do learn to settle down though they grow to like domesticity and become delightful mates and understanding companions.

To dress in harmony with their stars they will choose one or more of the following flowers, colors or jewels to compliment their wardrobe, but it is not essential that they do so. Flowers: mignonette, jessamine and yarrow. Colors: blue, violet and gray. Jewels: pearl, chrysolite, moonstone, lodestone and all unpolished blue and black gems.

They lack confidence but they have an excellent intuition. By putting more faith into their insight, and convincing themselves of their ability, they can succeed.

Those born between March 1st and March 9th—

Were most fortunate in having that jovial old man Jupiter dominant in the heavens at the time of their births. They are by nature warm, sympathetic and congenial. They should be able to attract powerfully influential people—and should achieve position and wealth.

They are also children of Neptune, and Neptune is a giver of gifts too, but they are aesthetic and artistic in nature. He makes his children highly emotional and given to enthusiasm—and at the same time danger-ously capable of self-deception.

They are easily influenced by others into intrigues and into secret alliances. As indicated by the symbol of their sign (which pictures an interesting position) they're seldom sure which way they're going.

The planetary colors indicated for them are sea-green, blue, purple (royal, of course) and violet-red. Their flowers are mignonette, jessamine and yarrow. Their gems: amethyst, emerald, sapphire and pearl.

One of the main problems of the average Piscean is lack of concentration, but these particular ones, having as they do, Jupiter as a dominant planet should experience no difficulty in overcoming this trait. They are wise enough to learn that life is a process not only of assimilation but of elimination as well, and they are equally wise enough to know what to eliminate, and let go all that is petty or unimportant.

Overindulgence is often their downfall. And colds are the ailments that can affect them most. They need fresh air but should conserve their energy.

Piscean natives usually go in for such lines as deal with the sea as shipping, and make excellent teachers and religious and social workers.

Neptune inclines them to artistic fields or imaginative writing. It may lead them to the theater or the movies. They should develop any talent that they may have along these or any aesthetic or inspirational line.

Jupiter, their dominant planet may help them to succeed in being judges, clergymen, lawyers, physicians or bankers—and has the added benefit of helping them attain any end they pursue.

Those born between March 10th and March 20th—

Will make some man a pleasing, comfortable, lovable husband. They by the nature of their sign, Pisces are sensitive, sympathetic, intuitive and agreeable. They have high ideals and fine feelings, and are interested, or SHOULD be, in all artistic and aesthetic, er, ah, things?

Many of them lack concentration and direction. Their dominant planet, Mars, does little to correct this. Frequently they have too many conflicting interests and this results in their scattering their forces. But they are restless and inattentive, physically and mentally. They'll ask questions, needless ones, not because they want an answer (they don't even wait for one), but just to give vent to a momentary whim.

The Pisces-born sometimes come under disorganizing elements that prevent him from realizing his full possibilities. This is bad enough in business, but with the Piscean it can also effect his love life. Their overly-demonstrative nature can result in a lack of response on the part of his partner.

The planetary colors of these Piscean natives are blood-red, red-violet, scarlet (if you've met one, you know it), mauve and lavender. Their flowers are mignonette, jessamine and yarrow. Their jewels are moonstone, crystal and pearl. Do pearls go well with basic lavender?

Mars, the warlike planet, was dominant in the heavens when these Pisceans were born, and they may bear some of Mars' characteristics, but hopefully tempered by the nature of their sign. They can gain courage, energy and strength from Mars, and these too can be used to subdue the less desirable traits. Unless they do they may find martial blitz instead of marital bliss.

Neptune the inspired is their ruling planet, though and enables them to appreciate the finer things in life.

But...he is the veiled one and indicates uncertainty, a tendency toward self-deception and a susceptibility to influence especially in *les affaires sexualles*. The combination of Neptune and Mars sometimes gives them strange ideas.

Mars rules soldiers, surgeons, dentists, chemists, barbers and iron and steel workers. Neptune governs artists, writers and all imaginative people and those connected with stage and screen. With these two powerful influences they'll find themselves engaged in many interesting pursuits. They will succeed too in foreign countries, or with anything that has to do with water, including the Navy!

EPILOGUE

And there you have it, girls. Of course, this is far from being a complete course in astrology. After all, I've known some queens who spent their whole lives looking after stars without ever getting off the ground.

As I've tried to make clear throughout the book, these notes are general, and only guidelines. You probably found some comments applicable to yourself, or to your sisters. But, if you want the complete picture, you would need a full personal chart made for your own horoscope. This means find a good astrologer in your town who'll need all kinds of information.

Whether you go this far with astrology or not, it can be useful, and fun. I have one dear friend who uses it regularly as a conversation opener with strangers. It works almost invariably. After all, you're offering to talk about the stranger's favorite subject, himself. And, for you scoffers, may I add that my friend has a high batting average in guessing the astrological sign from appearance and a few slim conversational clues.

But enough. I'm off to more earthy matters. There's a certain luminary who's joining me for dinner. With luck, I may have a shooting star on my hands—or on something.

ABOUT THE AUTHOR

VICTOR J. BANIS is the critically acclaimed author ("the master's touch in storytelling..."—*Publishers Weekly*) of more than 200 published books and numerous short stories in a career spanning nearly a half century. A native of Ohio and a longtime Californian, he lives and writes now in West Virginia's beautiful Blue Ridge.

You can visit him at http://www.vjbanis.com

www.ingramcontent.com/pod-product-compliance
Lightning Source LLC
Chambersburg PA
CBHW020001290326
41935CB00007B/265